C-2895 CAREER EXAMINATION SERIES

This is your
PASSBOOK for...

Public Safety Officer I

Test Preparation Study Guide
Questions & Answers

COPYRIGHT NOTICE

This book is SOLELY intended for, is sold ONLY to, and its use is RESTRICTED to individual, bona fide applicants or candidates who qualify by virtue of having seriously filed applications for appropriate license, certificate, professional and/or promotional advancement, higher school matriculation, scholarship, or other legitimate requirements of education and/or governmental authorities.

This book is NOT intended for use, class instruction, tutoring, training, duplication, copying, reprinting, excerption, or adaptation, etc., by:

1) Other publishers
2) Proprietors and/or Instructors of "Coaching" and/or Preparatory Courses
3) Personnel and/or Training Divisions of commercial, industrial, and governmental organizations
4) Schools, colleges, or universities and/or their departments and staffs, including teachers and other personnel
5) Testing Agencies or Bureaus
6) Study groups which seek by the purchase of a single volume to copy and/or duplicate and/or adapt this material for use by the group as a whole without having purchased individual volumes for each of the members of the group
7) Et al.

Such persons would be in violation of appropriate Federal and State statutes.

PROVISION OF LICENSING AGREEMENTS – Recognized educational, commercial, industrial, and governmental institutions and organizations, and others legitimately engaged in educational pursuits, including training, testing, and measurement activities, may address request for a licensing agreement to the copyright owners, who will determine whether, and under what conditions, including fees and charges, the materials in this book may be used them. In other words, a licensing facility exists for the legitimate use of the material in this book on other than an individual basis. However, it is asseverated and affirmed here that the material in this book CANNOT be used without the receipt of the express permission of such a licensing agreement from the Publishers. Inquiries re licensing should be addressed to the company, attention rights and permissions department.

All rights reserved, including the right of reproduction in whole or in part, in any form or by any means, electronic or mechanical, including photocopying, recording, or by any information storage and retrieval system, without permission in writing from the Publisher.

Copyright © 2024 by
National Learning Corporation

212 Michael Drive, Syosset, NY 11791
(516) 921-8888 • www.passbooks.com
E-mail: info@passbooks.com

PUBLISHED IN THE UNITED STATES OF AMERICA

PASSBOOK® SERIES

THE *PASSBOOK® SERIES* has been created to prepare applicants and candidates for the ultimate academic battlefield – the examination room.

At some time in our lives, each and every one of us may be required to take an examination – for validation, matriculation, admission, qualification, registration, certification, or licensure.

Based on the assumption that every applicant or candidate has met the basic formal educational standards, has taken the required number of courses, and read the necessary texts, the *PASSBOOK® SERIES* furnishes the one special preparation which may assure passing with confidence, instead of failing with insecurity. Examination questions – together with answers – are furnished as the basic vehicle for study so that the mysteries of the examination and its compounding difficulties may be eliminated or diminished by a sure method.

This book is meant to help you pass your examination provided that you qualify and are serious in your objective.

The entire field is reviewed through the huge store of content information which is succinctly presented through a provocative and challenging approach – the question-and-answer method.

A climate of success is established by furnishing the correct answers at the end of each test.

You soon learn to recognize types of questions, forms of questions, and patterns of questioning. You may even begin to anticipate expected outcomes.

You perceive that many questions are repeated or adapted so that you can gain acute insights, which may enable you to score many sure points.

You learn how to confront new questions, or types of questions, and to attack them confidently and work out the correct answers.

You note objectives and emphases, and recognize pitfalls and dangers, so that you may make positive educational adjustments.

Moreover, you are kept fully informed in relation to new concepts, methods, practices, and directions in the field.

You discover that you are actually taking the examination all the time: you are preparing for the examination by "taking" an examination, not by reading extraneous and/or supererogatory textbooks.

In short, this PASSBOOK®, used directedly, should be an important factor in helping you to pass your test.

PUBLIC SAFETY OFFICER I

DUTIES:
Learns and performs work in patrolling all Town properties, safeguarding Town buildings, grounds, equipment and other property owned, maintained or otherwise controlled by the Town, during all hours. Ensures the safety of people working, visitors, or otherwise using the premises. When applicable, enforces Town codes, rules and regulations. Performs related duties as required.

SCOPE OF THE EXAMINATION:
The written test designed to evaluate knowledge, skills and /or abilities in the following areas:
1. **Applying Written Information in a Safety and Security Setting** — These questions evaluate your ability to read, interpret and apply rules, regulations, directives, written narratives and other related material. You will be required to read a set of information and to appropriately apply the information to situations similar to those typically experienced in a public safety and security service setting. All information needed to answer the questions is contained in the rules, regulations, etc. which are cited.
2. **Following Directions (Maps)** — These questions test your ability to follow physical/geographic directions using street maps or building maps. You will have to read and understand a set of directions and then use them on a simple map.
3. **Preparing Written Material** — These questions test for the ability to present information clearly and accurately, and to organize paragraphs logically and comprehensibly. For some questions, you will be given information in two or three sentences followed by four restatements of the information. You must then choose the best version. For other questions, you will be given paragraphs with their sentences out of order. You must then choose, from four suggestions, the best order for the sentences.

INTRODUCTION

This test guide provides a general description of the most common subject areas which will be tested and an explanation of the different types of questions you may see on the test.

Not all subject areas tested in the Safety and Security Series are covered in this test guide. The Examination Announcement will list the subject areas that will be included on the particular test you will be taking. Some of these subject areas may not be covered in this test guide.

The most common subject areas included in the Safety and Security Series are:

1. **APPLYING WRITTEN INFORMATION IN A SAFETY AND SECURITY SETTING:** These questions evaluate your ability to read, interpret and apply rules, regulations, directions, written narratives and other related material. You will be required to read a set of information and to appropriately apply the information to situations similar to those typically experienced in a public safety and security service setting. All information needed to answer the questions is contained in the rules, regulations, etc. which are cited.

2. **FOLLOWING DIRECTIONS (MAPS):** These questions test your ability to follow physical/geographic directions using street maps or building maps. You will have to read and understand a set of directions and then use them on a simple map.

3. **PREPARING WRITTEN MATERIAL:** These questions test for the ability to present information clearly and accurately, and to organize paragraphs logically and comprehensibly. For some questions, you will be given information in two or three sentences, followed by four restatements of the information. You must then choose the best version. For other questions, you will be given paragraphs with their sentences out of order. You must then choose, from among four choices, the best order for the sentences.

4. **PRINCIPLES AND PRACTICES OF SAFETY AND SECURITY:** These questions test for a knowledge of the proper principles and practices in the field of safety and security. The questions will cover such areas as selecting the best course of action to take in a safety or security related situation.

5. **SAFETY AND SECURITY METHODS AND PROCEDURES:** These questions test for knowledge of the methods and procedures utilized in safety and security related positions. The questions cover such areas as principles and practices of safety and security precautions in a building or grounds setting, accident prevention, proper response to safety or security related incidents, the investigation of incidents, and the inspection of buildings or grounds for potential safety and/or security problems.

INTRODUCTION – CONTINUED

6. **UNDERSTANDING AND INTERPRETING WRITTEN MATERIAL:** These questions test how well you comprehend written material. You will be provided with brief reading selections and will be asked questions about the selections. All the information required to answer the questions will be presented in the selections; you will not be required to have any special knowledge relating to the subject areas of the selections.

7. **SUPERVISION:** These questions test for knowledge of the principles and practices employed in planning, organizing, and controlling the activities of a work unit toward predetermined objectives. The concepts covered, usually in a situational question format, include such topics as assigning and reviewing work; evaluating performance; maintaining work standards; motivating and developing subordinates; implementing procedural change; increasing efficiency; and dealing with problems of absenteeism, morale, and discipline.

8. **ADMINISTRATIVE SUPERVISION:** These questions test for knowledge of the principles and practices involved in directing the activities of a large subordinate staff, including subordinate supervisors. Questions relate to the personal interactions between an upper level supervisor and his/her subordinate supervisors in the accomplishment of objectives. These questions cover such areas as assigning work to and coordinating the activities of several units, establishing and guiding staff development programs, evaluating the performance of subordinate supervisors, and maintaining relationships with other organizational sections.

The remainder of this test guide explains how you will be tested in each subject area listed above. A **TEST TASK** is provided for each subject area. This is an explanation of how a question is presented and how to correctly answer it. Read each explanation carefully. This test guide also provides at least one **SAMPLE QUESTION** for each subject area. The sample question is similar to the type of questions that will be presented on the actual test. This test guide provides the **SOLUTION** and correct answer to each sample question. You should study each sample question and solution in order to understand how the correct answer was determined.

At the end of this test guide we have included a **PRACTICE TEST** which includes additional examples of the types of questions you may see on your written test. Answers are provided in the Practice Test Key so that you can see how well you have done.

SUBJECT AREA 1

APPLYING WRITTEN INFORMATION IN A SAFETY AND SECURITY SETTING: These questions evaluate your ability to read, interpret and apply rules, regulations, directions, written narratives and other related material. You will be required to read a set of information and to appropriately apply the information to situations similar to those typically experienced in a public safety and security service setting. All information needed to answer the questions is contained in the rules, regulations, etc. which are cited.

TEST TASK: You will be given a set of rules, regulations, or other written information to read. You will then be asked a question which requires you to apply the rule to a given situation.

SAMPLE QUESTION:

RULE: While patrolling your grounds or building, keep a notebook and pencil with you. Keep the following emergency phone numbers in the notebook: police, fire department, nearby hospitals, alarm company, your supervisor, and the head of your building.

When you observe something out of the ordinary, take notes. Describe what is unusual, people who are unfamiliar, and any suspicious activity. If a crime or offense takes place, record what happened, who was involved, physical appearance of the suspect, clothing worn by the suspect, time and date, names and phone numbers of witnesses, where suspect was last seen, and any physical evidence found.

SITUATION: While you are doing your rounds at 11:20 p.m. you notice a door that has been left ajar. The door opens to the office of the Assistant Director of your facility. The door is typically closed and locked for the day when the Assistant Director leaves, usually between 5:00 and 6:00 p.m. The office is dark and no one is there.

QUESTION: Based solely on the above Rule and Situation, what, if anything, should be recorded in your notebook?

A. The office was dark when you entered it.
B. No one was in the office.
C. The door was open at 11:20 p.m.
D. No entry needs to be made.

The correct answer to this sample question is choice C.

SOLUTION: *The Situation states that while doing your rounds at 11:20 p.m., you notice a door left ajar. This door is typically closed and locked for the day between 5:00 and 6:00 p.m. by the Assistant Director. The question asks what, if anything, you should record about this incident in your notebook. To answer the question, evaluate all of the choices.*

Solution continued on next page.

SUBJECT AREA 1 – CONTINUED

Choice A states that you should record in your notebook the fact that the office was dark when you entered it. The Rule states that you should take notes when you observe something out of the ordinary. It is not out of the ordinary for the Assistant Director's office to be dark at 11:20 p.m. since the Assistant Director usually leaves for the day between 5:00 and 6:00 p.m. Choice A is incorrect.

Choice B states that you should record in your notebook the fact that no one was in the office. The Rule states that you should take notes when you observe something out of the ordinary. It is not out of the ordinary for the Assistant Director's office to be unoccupied at 11:20 p.m. since the Assistant Director is not usually at work after 6:00 p.m. Choice B is incorrect.

Choice C states that you should record in your notebook the fact that the door was open at 11:20 p.m. The Rule states that you should take notes when you observe something out of the ordinary. It is out of the ordinary for the Assistant Director's office door to be open at 11:20 p.m. because the door is typically closed and locked when the Assistant Director leaves for the day, usually between 5:00 and 6:00 p.m. Choice C is the correct answer.

Choice D states that you should make no entry in your notebook. The Rule states that you should take notes when you observe something out of the ordinary. It is out of the ordinary for the Assistant Director's office door to be open at 11:20 p.m. because the door is typically closed and locked when the Assistant Director leaves for the day, usually between 5:00 and 6:00 p.m. Choice D is incorrect.

SUBJECT AREA 2

FOLLOWING DIRECTIONS (MAPS): These questions test your ability to follow physical/geographic directions using street maps or building maps. You will have to read and understand a set of directions and then use them on a simple map.

TEST TASK: You will be provided with street maps or building maps. You will then be asked questions which require you to refer to the given maps and related information.

SAMPLE QUESTION:

DIRECTIONS: Base your answer to the following question on the sample information and sample map below. The map below shows a section of a city. The circled numbers are starting points and stopping points. Buildings are shown with letters. A roadblock is shown as a dark circle. One-way blocks are shown with an arrow pointing in the direction that you may travel on that block. For example:

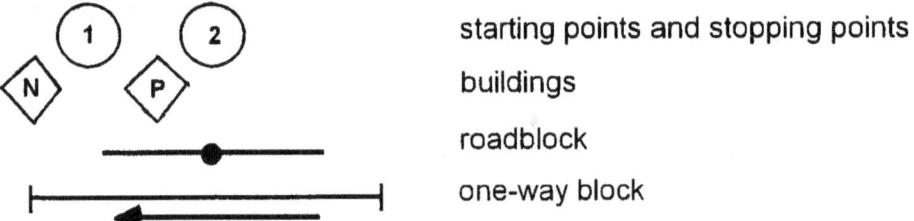

You may not go through a roadblock or travel in the wrong direction on a one-way block. You are to answer the question by finding and following the SHORTEST CORRECT route between the two locations given. All blocks are equal in length.

NOTE 1: Blocks may be traveled in either direction UNLESS only one direction is shown by an arrow for that block.

NOTE 2: You "pass" a building when you travel the block NEAREST the building.

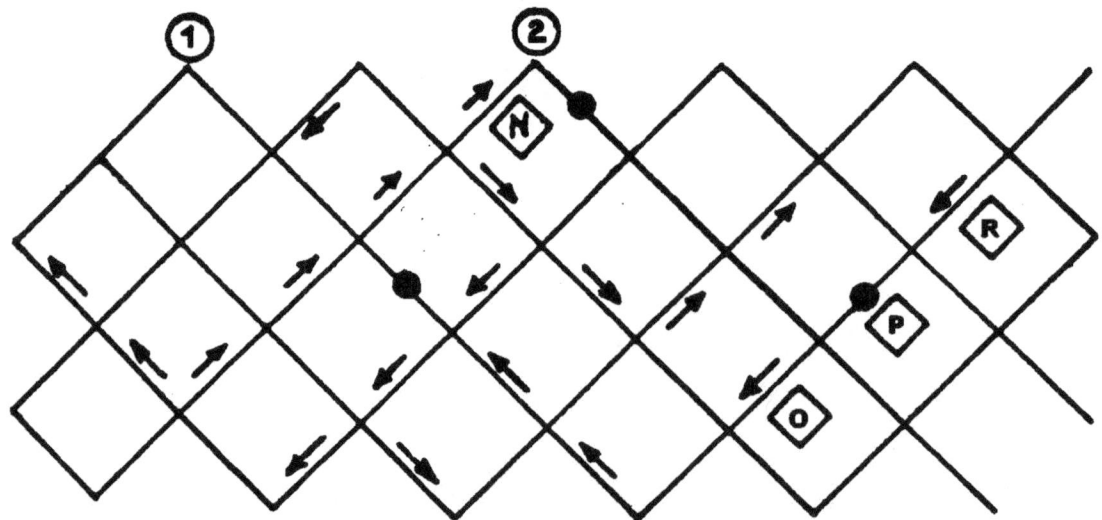

SUBJECT AREA 2 – CONTINUED

QUESTION: Which one of the following is a building you pass on the shortest correct route from point 1 to point 2?

A. N
B. O
C. P
D. R

The correct answer to this sample question is choice A.

SOLUTION:

Choice A is the correct answer to this question. The shortest correct route from point 1 to point 2 is four blocks and passes only building N.

Choice B is not correct. You do not pass building O on the shortest correct route from point 1 to point 2.

Choice C is not correct. You do not pass building P on the shortest correct route from point 1 to point 2.

Choice D is not correct. You do not pass building R on the shortest correct route from point 1 to point 2.

SUBJECT AREA 3

PREPARING WRITTEN MATERIAL: These questions test for the ability to present information clearly and accurately and for the ability to organize paragraphs logically and comprehensibly.

TEST TASK: There are two separate test tasks in this subject area.

- For the first, **Information Presentation**, you will be given information in two or three sentences, followed by four restatements of the information. You must then choose the best version.

- For the second, **Paragraph Organization**, you will be given paragraphs with their sentences out of order, and then be asked to choose, from among four choices, the best order for the sentences.

INFORMATION PRESENTATION SAMPLE QUESTION:

Martin Wilson failed to take proper precautions. His failure to take proper precautions caused a personal injury accident.

Which one of the following best presents the information above?

A. Martin Wilson failed to take proper precautions that caused a personal injury accident.
B. Proper precautions, which Martin Wilson failed to take, caused a personal injury accident.
C. Martin Wilson's failure to take proper precautions caused a personal injury accident.
D. Martin Wilson, who failed to take proper precautions, was in a personal injury accident.

The correct answer to this sample question is choice C.

SOLUTION:

Choice A conveys the incorrect impression that proper precautions caused a personal injury accident.

Choice B conveys the incorrect impression that proper precautions caused a personal injury accident.

Choice C best presents the original information: Martin Wilson failed to take proper precautions and this failure caused a personal injury accident.

Choice D states that Martin Wilson was in a personal injury accident. The original information states that Martin Wilson caused a personal injury accident, but it does not state that Martin Wilson was in a personal injury accident.

SUBJECT AREA 3 – CONTINUED

PARAGRAPH ORGANIZATION SAMPLE QUESTION:

The following question is based upon a group of sentences. The sentences are shown out of sequence, but when correctly arranged, they form a connected, well-organized paragraph. Read the sentences, and then answer the question about the best arrangement of these sentences.

1. Eventually, they piece all of this information together and make a choice.

2. Before actually deciding upon a human services job, people usually think about several possibilities.

3. They imagine themselves in different situations, and in so doing, they probably think about their interests, goals, and abilities.

4. Choosing among occupations in the field of human services is an important decision to make.

Which one of the following is the best arrangement of these sentences?

A. 2-4-1-3
B. 2-3-4-1
C. 4-2-1-3
D. 4-2-3-1

The correct answer to this sample question is choice D.

SOLUTION:

Choices A and C present the information in the paragraph out of logical sequence. In both A and C, sentence 1 comes before sentence 3. The key element in the organization of this paragraph is that sentence 3 contains the information to which sentence 1 refers; therefore, in logical sequence, sentence 3 should come before sentence 1.

Choice B also presents the information in the paragraph out of logical sequence. Choice B places the main idea of the paragraph (Sentence 4) in between two detail sentences (Sentences 1 and 3). The logical sequence of the information presented in the paragraph is therefore interrupted.

Choice D presents the information in the paragraph in the best logical sequence. Sentence 4 introduces the main idea of the paragraph: "choosing an occupation in the field of human services." Sentences 2-3-1 then follow up on this idea by describing, in order, the steps involved in making such a choice. Choice D is the best answer to this sample question.

SUBJECT AREA 4

PRINCIPLES AND PRACTICES OF SAFETY AND SECURITY: These questions test for a knowledge of the proper principles and practices in the field of safety and security. The questions will cover such areas as selecting the best course of action to take in a safety or security related situation.

TEST TASK: You will be presented with situations in which you must apply knowledge of the principles and practices of safety and security to answer the questions correctly.

SAMPLE QUESTION:

You are in charge of maintaining order in a room where a large number of people gather to transact business. A woman in the back of one of the lines starts to shout that she has been waiting for an hour and her line "has not moved at all." She continues to protest, and the rest of the crowd is getting restless.

Which one of the following actions would be best to take first in this situation?

A. Escort the woman to the head of the line and make sure her business is transacted promptly.
B. Tell the woman that unless she acts in a more orderly fashion, you will escort her out of the room.
C. Immediately remove the woman from the room.
D. Call the local police and detain the woman until the police arrive.

The correct answer to this sample question is choice B.

SOLUTION:

Choice A is not correct because escorting the woman to the head of the line and making sure her business is transacted promptly is not the best action to take first in this situation. This action could increase the restlessness of the other people who have also been waiting in the same line and will only serve to reinforce the woman's disruptive behavior.

Choice B is the correct answer because telling the woman that unless she acts in a more orderly fashion, you will escort her out of the room is the best action to take first in this situation. This action provides the woman with a clear warning to stop her disruptive behavior and advises her of the consequence should she continue to loudly protest the long wait.

Choice C is not correct because immediately removing the woman from the room is not the best action to take first in this situation. This action is too harsh based on the situation and could escalate the woman's disruptive behavior.

Choice D is not correct because calling the local police and detaining the woman until they arrive is not the best action to take first in this situation. This action is too harsh based on the situation and could escalate the woman's disruptive behavior.

SUBJECT AREA 5

SAFETY AND SECURITY METHODS AND PROCEDURES: These questions test for knowledge of the methods and procedures utilized in safety and security related positions. The questions cover such areas as principles and practices of safety and security precautions in a building or grounds setting, accident prevention, proper response to safety or security related incidents, the investigation of incidents, and the inspection of buildings or grounds for potential safety and/or security problems.

TEST TASK: You will be presented with questions in which you must apply knowledge of the methods and procedures utilized in safety and security related positions to answer the questions correctly.

SAMPLE QUESTION:

The most important purpose of patrolling the halls and grounds of a facility is to

A. discourage potential violations of rules or laws
B. give people on site the opportunity to obtain information or advice
C. maintain a routine observation of facility employees and their actions for your records
D. be able to provide assistance to local police authorities by accurately reporting whether unauthorized activity occurs in or near the facility

The correct answer to this sample question is choice A.

SOLUTION:

Choice A *is the correct answer because discouraging potential violations of rules or laws is the most important purpose of patrolling the halls and grounds of a facility. Your presence while patrolling the halls and grounds of a facility may be enough to deter potential rule or law violators.*

Choice B *is not correct because giving people on site the opportunity to obtain information or advice is not the most important purpose of patrolling the halls and grounds of a facility. Although giving people on site the opportunity to obtain information or advice may be an important purpose of patrolling the halls and grounds of a facility, it is not the* most *important purpose.*

Choice C *is not correct because maintaining a routine observation of facility employees and their actions for your records is not the most important purpose of patrolling the halls and grounds of a facility. Although maintaining a routine observation of facility employees and their actions for your records may be an important purpose of patrolling the halls and grounds of a facility, it is not the* most *important purpose.*

Choice D *is not correct because being able to provide assistance to local police authorities by accurately reporting whether unauthorized activity occurs in or near the facility is not the most important purpose of patrolling the halls and grounds of a facility. Although being able to provide assistance to local police authorities by accurately reporting whether unauthorized activity occurs in or near the facility may be an important purpose of patrolling the halls and grounds of a facility, it is not the* most *important purpose.*

SUBJECT AREA 6

UNDERSTANDING AND INTERPRETING WRITTEN MATERIAL: These questions test how well you comprehend written material. You will be provided with brief reading selections and will be asked questions about the selections. All the information required to answer the questions will be presented in the selections; you will not be required to have any special knowledge relating to the subject areas of the selections.

TEST TASK: You will be provided with brief reading passages and then will be asked questions relating to the passages. All the information required to answer the questions will be provided in the passages.

SAMPLE QUESTION: "Increasingly, behavior termed 'road rage' is being viewed as a public health issue, because of the number of deaths and injuries related to it. Such behavior is often a reaction to the feeling that one has been treated unfairly by another driver, and it is much less likely to occur if a driver is treated fairly. 'Fair play' on the road includes the observance not only of traffic regulations but also of the rules of courtesy. Courteous driving is based on common sense consideration for other drivers and a strong desire to make the roads safe for everyone. Good highway manners should become just as much a matter of habit as other kinds of manners."

Which one of the following statements is best supported by the above selection?

A. Courteous driving contributes to road safety.
B. Those who are generally polite are also courteous drivers.
C. Unlike driving courtesy, the observance of traffic regulations is a matter of habit.
D. Being courteous when driving is more important than observing traffic regulations.

The correct answer to this sample question is choice A.

SOLUTION: To answer this question correctly, you must evaluate each choice against the written selection and determine the one that is best supported by the written selection.

Choice A *states, "Courteous driving contributes to road safety." Choice A is supported by the statement in the written selection that, "Courteous driving is based on...a strong desire to make the roads safe for everyone." This is the correct answer.*

Choice B *states, "Those who are generally polite are also courteous drivers." Choice B is not supported by the written selection. The written selection does not mention "those who are generally polite" at all. Choice B is not the correct answer to this question.*

Choice C *states, "Unlike driving courtesy, the observance of traffic regulations is a matter of habit." Choice C is not supported by the written selection. The written selection makes no such bold statement. Instead, the written material mildly suggests that "Good highway manners should become just as much a matter of habit as other kinds of manners." Choice C is not the correct answer to this question.*

Choice D *states, "Being courteous when driving is more important than observing traffic regulations." Choice D is not supported by the written selection. The written selection states, "'Fair play' on the road includes the observance not only of traffic regulations but also of the rules of courtesy." The written selection does not state that being courteous is more important than observing traffic regulations. Choice D is not the correct answer to this question.*

SUBJECT AREA 7

SUPERVISION: These questions test for knowledge of the principles and practices employed in planning, organizing, and controlling the activities of a work unit toward predetermined objectives. The concepts covered, usually in a situational question format, include such topics as assigning and reviewing work; evaluating performance; maintaining work standards; motivating and developing subordinates; implementing procedural change; increasing efficiency; and dealing with problems of absenteeism, morale, and discipline.

TEST TASK: You will be presented with situations in which you must apply knowledge of the principles and practices of supervision in order to answer the questions correctly.

SAMPLE QUESTION:
Assume that the unit you supervise is given a new work assignment and that you are unsure about the proper procedure to use in performing this assignment. Which one of the following actions should you take FIRST in this situation?

A. Obtain input from your staff.
B. Consult other unit supervisors who have had similar assignments.
C. Use an appropriate procedure from a similar assignment that you are familiar with.
D. Discuss the matter with your supervisor.

The correct answer to this sample question is choice D.

SOLUTION:

Choice A is not correct. Since this assignment is new for your unit, your staff would not be expected to be more knowledgeable than you about the proper procedure.

Choice B is not correct. Although discussing this matter with other supervisors may increase your knowledge of the new assignment, similar assignments performed in other units may differ in some important way from your new assignment. Other units may also function differently from your unit, so the procedures used to perform similar assignments may differ accordingly.

Choice C is not correct. Since this assignment is new for your unit, you would have no way of knowing whether the procedure from a similar assignment is appropriate to use. You would need someone with the appropriate knowledge, usually your supervisor, to determine if the procedure from a similar assignment could be used before you actually employed this procedure in the performance of your new assignment.

Choice D is the correct answer to this question. Your supervisor is more likely to be informed about what procedure may be appropriate for work that he or she assigns to you than would other unit supervisors or your staff. Even if your supervisor does not know what procedure is appropriate, a decision regarding which procedure to use should be made with his or her participation, since he or she has the ultimate responsibility for your unit's work.

SUBJECT AREA 8

ADMINISTRATIVE SUPERVISION: These questions test for knowledge of the principles and practices involved in directing the activities of a large subordinate staff, including subordinate supervisors. Questions relate to the personal interactions between an upper level supervisor and his/her subordinate supervisors in the accomplishment of objectives. These questions cover such areas as assigning work to and coordinating the activities of several units, establishing and guiding staff development programs, evaluating the performance of subordinate supervisors, and maintaining relationships with other organizational sections.

TEST TASK: You will be presented with situations in which you must apply knowledge of the principles and practices of administrative supervision to answer the questions correctly. You will be placed in the role of a supervisor of a section, which is made up of several units. Each unit has a supervisor and several employees. All unit supervisors report directly to you.

SAMPLE QUESTION:

You have delegated a work project to two unit supervisors and have asked them to collaborate on it. Later, you observe two employees strongly arguing about which one of them is responsible for a certain activity within the work project. The arguing employees work for different units. Which one of the following actions is most appropriate for you to take in this situation?

A. Intercede in the employees' argument and settle it.
B. Meet with the unit supervisors of the two employees and inform them of the situation you observed.
C. Inform one unit supervisor of the situation and ask this supervisor to take care of it.
D. Set up a meeting that includes both unit supervisors and both employees to resolve the situation.

The correct answer to this sample question is choice B.

SOLUTION:

Choice A is not correct. In your position, you supervise properly by giving direction through your unit supervisors. By taking this choice, you are not allowing your unit supervisors to handle a problem involving their staff members. Also, it is not reasonable that you would be able to settle the employees' dispute. Earlier, you delegated the work project to the two unit supervisors, who would be responsible for assigning activities related to the project. The two unit supervisors must deal with the problem.

Choice B is the correct answer to this question. The two unit supervisors are collaborating on the work project and therefore giving the assignments. You should meet with them and tell them about the employees' argument. The unit supervisors should be informed about the point of contention and the fact that the two employees had a heated argument. The unit supervisors must then work out a way to handle the situation.

Choice C is not correct. Speaking to only one supervisor about the situation means that the second supervisor may be uninformed, or only partly informed, about the situation. You cannot be assured that the first supervisor will include the second supervisor in finding a way to settle the issue. If the first unit supervisor chooses to handle the situation on his own and speak to both employees, this supervisor would be giving direction to one employee from another unit. This is not good supervisory practice. Also, in taking Choice C, you are favoring one supervisor and slighting the other.

Choice D is not correct. The unit supervisors need to come up with a way of handling the situation that you observed. To do this, they must be informed without the employees present. Also, by including the employees in the meeting, you may get a replay of their earlier argument, which is not helpful.

PRACTICE TEST

Below and on the following pages are additional examples of the types of questions that will be on the written test for the Safety and Security Series. The answers are given on page 25. Good luck!

APPLYING WRITTEN INFORMATION IN A SAFETY AND SECURITY SETTING

DIRECTIONS: The following two questions evaluate your ability to read and interpret a specific rule and apply it to a given situation or situations. Each question or set of questions is given with a **RULE** along with a **SITUATION** or situations. You should base your answers to these questions upon the information provided and **NOT** upon any other information you may have on the subject.

1. **RULE:** A security officer is to obey all lawful regulations of the employer and all orders of a police officer in police matters. The security officer is to assist and cooperate with police officers in preserving the peace. Where police are on the scene, on duty and off duty security personnel should identify themselves as security officers and offer assistance. The police officer's directives and judgment shall prevail.

SITUATION: When leaving work for the day, you see that a motor vehicle accident has taken place on the highway near your workplace. You approach the accident in your car and see that a police officer is on the scene. You inform the police officer that you are a security officer. Traffic is stopped.

According to the above Rule, under which one of the following conditions, if any, should you take control of directing traffic in this Situation?

A. The police officer instructs you to direct traffic.
B. You regularly direct traffic as part of your job.
C. You should not direct traffic because you are off duty.
D. You should not direct traffic because the highway is not on facility property.

2. **RULE:** If a law enforcement officer is required to be at a mental health facility, the officer will be required to lock his weapon in a designated gun cabinet and retain the only key. In areas where gun cabinets are not available, the law enforcement officer shall be asked to remove the bullets from his weapon and retain the weapon. The only other allowable option is for the officer to lock the weapon in his patrol car.

SITUATION: During rounds as a security officer in a mental health facility with no gun control cabinets available, you come upon a law enforcement officer whom you know to be a firearms instructor. You allow the officer to enter the building with his weapon.

Based solely on the above Rule and Situation, in which one of the following cases is your action correct?

A. The officer has stated that his police agency prohibits an officer from locking a weapon in his patrol car.
B. The officer has stated that he would be willing to put his weapon in a gun cabinet.
C. The officer has shown you a letter stating he must attend a meeting at the facility today on the topic of firearm instruction.
D. The officer has removed the bullets from his weapon.

FOLLOWING DIRECTIONS (MAPS)

DIRECTIONS: The following map presents a diagram of a floor of an office building. You should become familiar with the map and interpret it with the legend provided. Use the map to answer the questions on the next page.

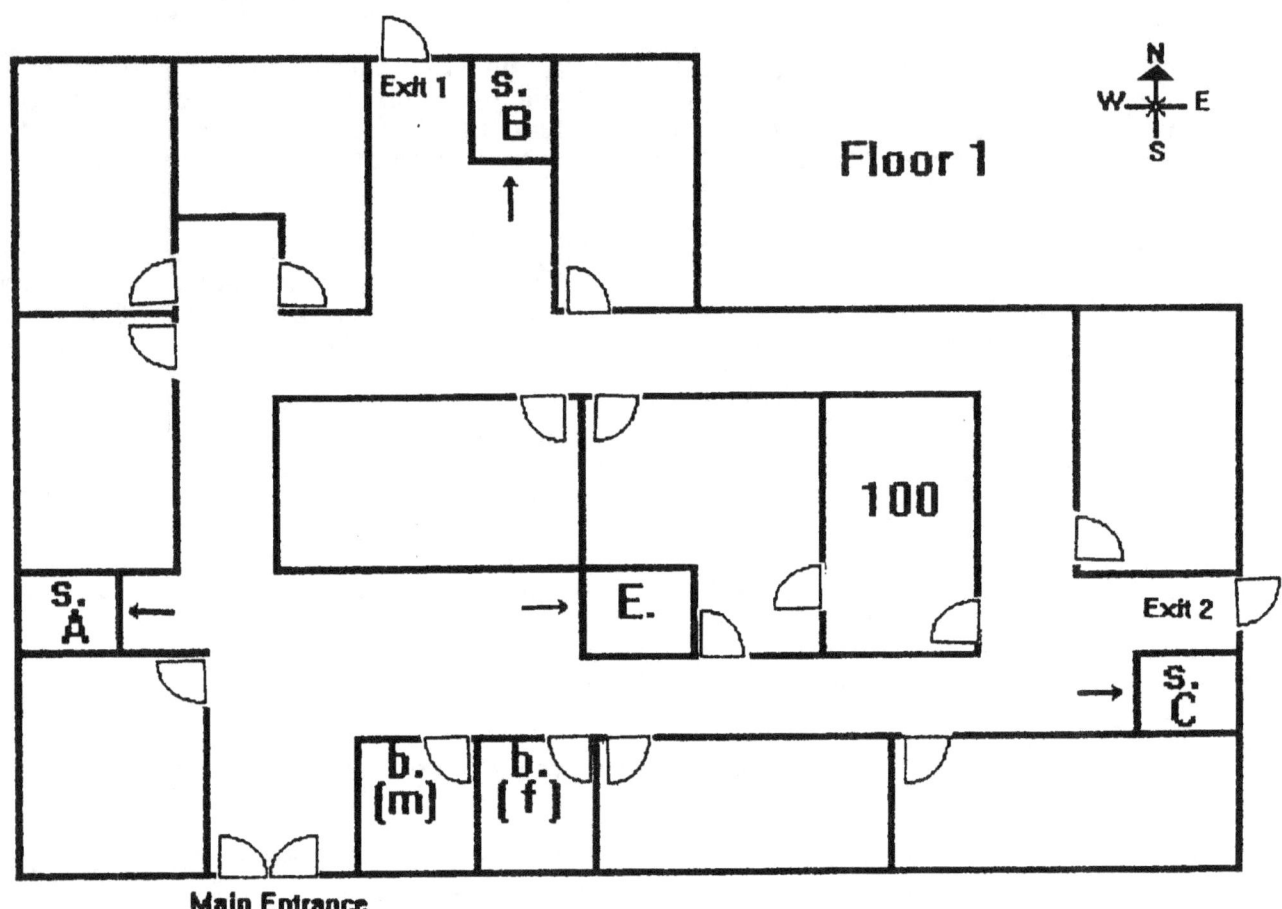

Legend:

Office Numbers appear inside the rooms; e.g., 100 = Office No. 100

E. = Elevator
s. = Stairwell; e.g., s.C = Stairwell C
b. = bathroom; e.g., b.(m) = bathroom (male)
           b.(f) = bathroom (female)

Assume that people receiving directions are able-bodied unless otherwise noted.

→ = the entrance to a stairwell or elevator used to access other floors in the building

◐ or ◑ = doors to an office or the building

FOLLOWING DIRECTIONS (MAPS) (Continued)

3. For a person in Office No. 100, which one of the following is the most direct route to leave the building in an emergency?

A. through exit 1
B. through exit 2
C. through stairwell C
D. through the Main Entrance

4. Which one of the following routes is the best to take if the elevator is out of service and a person standing directly inside the main entrance wants to get from Floor 1 to Floor 2 in the most efficient way?

A. Walk straight, take the second right, take the first left and take stairwell B to the second floor.
B. Walk straight, take the second right, walk straight, take the next right, take the first left and take stairwell C to the second floor.
C. Walk straight, take the first right, walk straight and take stairwell C to the second floor.
D. Walk straight, take the first left and take stairwell A to the second floor.

PREPARING WRITTEN MATERIAL

DIRECTIONS: Read the information given in the following two questions carefully. Then select the choice which presents the information most clearly, accurately, and completely.

5. Senator Martinez met with the county legislature. Then Senator Martinez announced that the meal subsidy program would start in June.

Which one of the following best presents the information given above?

A. After meeting with the county legislature, Senator Martinez announced that the meal subsidy program would start in June.
B. Senator Martinez met with the county legislature and announced that the meal subsidy program would start in June.
C. Senator Martinez announced that the meal subsidy program would start in June after a meeting with the county legislature.
D. Senator Martinez, who met with the county legislature, announced that the meal subsidy program would start in June.

6. Frank Colombe wrote the press release. He sent three copies to the Director. The Director then gave one of the copies to the Commissioner.

Which one of the following best presents the information given above?

A. Frank Colombe sent to the Director three copies of the press release he had written, who then gave a copy to the Commissioner.
B. Frank Colombe sent three copies of the press release he had written to the Director, who then gave one of the copies to the Commissioner.
C. The Director gave the Commissioner one of the three copies of the press release Frank Colombe had written and had been sent to him.
D. Of the three copies of the press release Frank Colombe had written and sent to the Director, one was then given to the Commissioner by him.

PREPARING WRITTEN MATERIAL (Continued)

DIRECTIONS: The following two (2) questions are based upon a group of sentences. The sentences are shown out of sequence, but when they are correctly arranged they form a connected, well-organized paragraph. Read the sentences and then answer the question about what order to arrange them in.

7.
1. The phosphates in detergents are carried into sewage systems, and from there into local rivers and streams, and eventually into large bodies of water.

2. The algae absorb much of the available oxygen that is necessary to sustain marine life.

3. There is no doubt that phosphates damage the environment through a complex chain of events.

4. Phosphates are nutrients, and, as such, they aid the growth of the algae living in the water.

5. This results not only in the death of fish and other aquatic life, but also in the too-thick growth of vegetation in the water.

Which one of the following is the best arrangement of these sentences?

A. 1-3-4-2-5
B. 1-4-2-5-3
C. 3-1-4-2-5
D. 3-4-2-1-5

8.
1. Never before has time been measured at a speed beyond the realm of experience.

2. Just how profound an effect it is having on society is as yet to be determined.

3. The computer has accelerated our sense of time beyond anything we have experienced before.

4. Though it is possible to conceive of an interval that brief and even to manipulate time at that speed, it is not possible to experience it.

5. It works in a time frame in which the nanosecond—a billionth of a second—is the primary measurement.

Which one of the following is the best arrangement of these sentences?

A. 1-2-3-5-4
B. 1-4-3-5-2
C. 3-2-5-4-1
D. 3-5-4-1-2

PRINCIPLES AND PRACTICES OF SAFETY AND SECURITY

9. You are on patrol in a radio-equipped car at night. You discover that a large drum of gasoline near a garage on the property is punctured and is rapidly spilling gasoline on the ground around the building.

Which one of the following actions should you take first in this situation?

A. Submit a written report of the incident to your supervisor.
B. Report the matter to headquarters.
C. Examine the puncture to see if it was accidental or deliberate.
D. Check other drums or containers around the building for punctures.

10. You hear shouting on the second floor of a building where you are on duty. Upon arriving at the scene, you see two building employees engaged in a fist fight in the hall.

Which one of the following actions should you take first in this situation?

A. Report the matter to the supervisors of the two employees.
B. Ask observers how the fight started.
C. Call for assistance.
D. Break up the fight.

SAFETY AND SECURITY METHODS AND PROCEDURES

11. Complaints relating to suspicious activity, especially at night, are often groundless. Which one of the following is the best way of handling such a complaint?

A. Analyze the nature of the complaint to make sure that it is justifiable before dispatching anyone to the scene.
B. Consider the complaint justified only if it corresponds to similar complaints in the same area.
C. Take no action on the complaint, but make a record of it.
D. Attend to the complaint immediately on the assumption that it is justified.

12. In the course of an investigation, you are interviewing a person who is over-talkative. Which one of the following is the best method for you to use in order to obtain the facts which you seek?

A. Tell the witness to talk only about the facts you are interested in.
B. Place a time limit on the witness's answers to your questions.
C. Make it clear that you want only "yes" or "no" answers to your questions.
D. Guide the conversation toward the subject of interest when the witness talks about subjects clearly not relevant to the interview.

UNDERSTANDING AND INTERPRETING WRITTEN MATERIAL

DIRECTIONS: The following two questions are related to the reading selection preceding each question. Base your answer to the question SOLELY on what is said in the selection – NOT on what you may happen to know about the subject discussed.

13. "The increasing demands upon our highways from a growing population and the development of forms of transportation not anticipated when the highways were first built have brought about congestion, confusion, and conflict, until the yearly toll of traffic accidents is now at an appalling level. If the death and disaster that traffic accidents bring throughout the year were concentrated into one calamity, we would shudder at the tremendous catastrophe. The loss is no less catastrophic because it is spread out over time and space."

Which one of the following statements concerning the yearly toll of traffic accidents is best supported by the passage above?

A. It is increasing the demands for safer means of transportation.
B. It has resulted in increased congestion, confusion, and conflict on our highways.
C. It has resulted mainly from the new forms of transportation.
D. It does not shock us as much as it should because the accidents do not all occur at the same time.

14. "Depression is one of the top public health problems in the United States, and its occurrence is on the rise. One in 20 Americans develops a case of depression serious enough to require professional treatment. The incidence of depression has been escalating among Baby Boomers (Americans born in the years 1946 through 1964). The reason for this increase is that the lifestyles of this generation have become increasingly demanding while offering little support. Also, stress and poor eating habits are now more the rule than the exception, and both can disrupt brain chemistry enough to bring on depression."

Which one of the following statements is best supported by the above selection?

A. We can expect a small proportion of the population to require treatment for depression at some time in their lives.
B. Baby Boomers have the highest rate of depression in the United States.
C. Lifestyle demands are the major cause of depression in the current generation.
D. Depression can cause a disruption in the chemistry of the brain.

SUPERVISION

DIRECTIONS: For the following two questions, assume that you are the newly appointed supervisor of a unit consisting of several employees. You report to a section head.

15. You have a suspicion that some of your employees are not working to the best of their abilities. Which one of the following actions should you take first in this situation?

A. Arrange for these employees to take a course in organizing priorities.
B. Determine which employee is the worst offender.
C. Assess the assignments and work methods of these employees.
D. Set up a meeting with these employees to learn about any work problems they are having.

16. As you are giving an employee a certain assignment, she expresses concern that it is too difficult. The employee is reluctant to accept the assignment. Which one of the following actions should you take first in this situation?

A. Insist that the employee take on the assignment.
B. Tell the employee that it is likely she has completed assignments of similar difficulty before.
C. Offer to share the tasks of the assignment with the employee.
D. Ask the employee why she sees the assignment as difficult.

ADMINISTRATIVE SUPERVISION

DIRECTIONS: For the following two questions, assume that you supervise a section composed of several units. Each unit has a supervisor and several employees. All unit supervisors report directly to you.

17. Assume that you are the head of a section made up of four units, each of which is responsible for similar work. The work volume of one of the units of the section has permanently decreased to the point that the supervisor of that unit now is responsible for much less work than any of the other three unit supervisors. Of the following, which determination should you as the section head make first in this situation?

A. Can other or additional tasks be assigned to this unit?
B. Can the unit supervisor function as assistant section head?
C. Can the unit supervisor's position be reclassified or reallocated?
D. Can the section be reorganized into three units?

18. In which one of the following circumstances should you try to reduce turnover in the section you supervise?

A. The turnover is higher than that of other sections.
B. The turnover reduces the number of highly experienced employees.
C. The turnover lowers the efficiency of the section.
D. The turnover requires unit supervisors to spend a moderate amount of time in training new employees.

PRACTICE TEST KEY

(1) A
(2) D
(3) B
(4) D
(5) A
(6) B
(7) C
(8) D
(9) B
(10) C
(11) D
(12) D
(13) D
(14) A
(15) C
(16) D
(17) A
(18) C

HOW TO TAKE A TEST

I. YOU MUST PASS AN EXAMINATION

A. *WHAT EVERY CANDIDATE SHOULD KNOW*

Examination applicants often ask us for help in preparing for the written test. What can I study in advance? What kinds of questions will be asked? How will the test be given? How will the papers be graded?

As an applicant for a civil service examination, you may be wondering about some of these things. Our purpose here is to suggest effective methods of advance study and to describe civil service examinations.

Your chances for success on this examination can be increased if you know how to prepare. Those "pre-examination jitters" can be reduced if you know what to expect. You can even experience an adventure in good citizenship if you know why civil service exams are given.

B. *WHY ARE CIVIL SERVICE EXAMINATIONS GIVEN?*

Civil service examinations are important to you in two ways. As a citizen, you want public jobs filled by employees who know how to do their work. As a job seeker, you want a fair chance to compete for that job on an equal footing with other candidates. The best-known means of accomplishing this two-fold goal is the competitive examination.

Exams are widely publicized throughout the nation. They may be administered for jobs in federal, state, city, municipal, town or village governments or agencies.

Any citizen may apply, with some limitations, such as the age or residence of applicants. Your experience and education may be reviewed to see whether you meet the requirements for the particular examination. When these requirements exist, they are reasonable and applied consistently to all applicants. Thus, a competitive examination may cause you some uneasiness now, but it is your privilege and safeguard.

C. *HOW ARE CIVIL SERVICE EXAMS DEVELOPED?*

Examinations are carefully written by trained technicians who are specialists in the field known as "psychological measurement," in consultation with recognized authorities in the field of work that the test will cover. These experts recommend the subject matter areas or skills to be tested; only those knowledges or skills important to your success on the job are included. The most reliable books and source materials available are used as references. Together, the experts and technicians judge the difficulty level of the questions.

Test technicians know how to phrase questions so that the problem is clearly stated. Their ethics do not permit "trick" or "catch" questions. Questions may have been tried out on sample groups, or subjected to statistical analysis, to determine their usefulness.

Written tests are often used in combination with performance tests, ratings of training and experience, and oral interviews. All of these measures combine to form the best-known means of finding the right person for the right job.

II. HOW TO PASS THE WRITTEN TEST

A. NATURE OF THE EXAMINATION

To prepare intelligently for civil service examinations, you should know how they differ from school examinations you have taken. In school you were assigned certain definite pages to read or subjects to cover. The examination questions were quite detailed and usually emphasized memory. Civil service exams, on the other hand, try to discover your present ability to perform the duties of a position, plus your potentiality to learn these duties. In other words, a civil service exam attempts to predict how successful you will be. Questions cover such a broad area that they cannot be as minute and detailed as school exam questions.

In the public service similar kinds of work, or positions, are grouped together in one "class." This process is known as *position-classification*. All the positions in a class are paid according to the salary range for that class. One class title covers all of these positions, and they are all tested by the same examination.

B. FOUR BASIC STEPS

1) Study the announcement

How, then, can you know what subjects to study? Our best answer is: "Learn as much as possible about the class of positions for which you've applied." The exam will test the knowledge, skills and abilities needed to do the work.

Your most valuable source of information about the position you want is the official exam announcement. This announcement lists the training and experience qualifications. Check these standards and apply only if you come reasonably close to meeting them.

The brief description of the position in the examination announcement offers some clues to the subjects which will be tested. Think about the job itself. Review the duties in your mind. Can you perform them, or are there some in which you are rusty? Fill in the blank spots in your preparation.

Many jurisdictions preview the written test in the exam announcement by including a section called "Knowledge and Abilities Required," "Scope of the Examination," or some similar heading. Here you will find out specifically what fields will be tested.

2) Review your own background

Once you learn in general what the position is all about, and what you need to know to do the work, ask yourself which subjects you already know fairly well and which need improvement. You may wonder whether to concentrate on improving your strong areas or on building some background in your fields of weakness. When the announcement has specified "some knowledge" or "considerable knowledge," or has used adjectives like "beginning principles of…" or "advanced … methods," you can get a clue as to the number and difficulty of questions to be asked in any given field. More questions, and hence broader coverage, would be included for those subjects which are more important in the work. Now weigh your strengths and weaknesses against the job requirements and prepare accordingly.

3) Determine the level of the position

Another way to tell how intensively you should prepare is to understand the level of the job for which you are applying. Is it the entering level? In other words, is this the position in which beginners in a field of work are hired? Or is it an intermediate or advanced level? Sometimes this is indicated by such words as "Junior" or "Senior" in the class title. Other jurisdictions use Roman numerals to designate the level – Clerk I, Clerk II, for example. The word "Supervisor" sometimes appears in the title. If the level is not indicated by the title, check the description of duties. Will you be working under very close supervision, or will you have responsibility for independent decisions in this work?

4) Choose appropriate study materials

Now that you know the subjects to be examined and the relative amount of each subject to be covered, you can choose suitable study materials. For beginning level jobs, or even advanced ones, if you have a pronounced weakness in some aspect of your training, read a modern, standard textbook in that field. Be sure it is up to date and has general coverage. Such books are normally available at your library, and the librarian will be glad to help you locate one. For entry-level positions, questions of appropriate difficulty are chosen -- neither highly advanced questions, nor those too simple. Such questions require careful thought but not advanced training.

If the position for which you are applying is technical or advanced, you will read more advanced, specialized material. If you are already familiar with the basic principles of your field, elementary textbooks would waste your time. Concentrate on advanced textbooks and technical periodicals. Think through the concepts and review difficult problems in your field.

These are all general sources. You can get more ideas on your own initiative, following these leads. For example, training manuals and publications of the government agency which employs workers in your field can be useful, particularly for technical and professional positions. A letter or visit to the government department involved may result in more specific study suggestions, and certainly will provide you with a more definite idea of the exact nature of the position you are seeking.

III. KINDS OF TESTS

Tests are used for purposes other than measuring knowledge and ability to perform specified duties. For some positions, it is equally important to test ability to make adjustments to new situations or to profit from training. In others, basic mental abilities not dependent on information are essential. Questions which test these things may not appear as pertinent to the duties of the position as those which test for knowledge and information. Yet they are often highly important parts of a fair examination. For very general questions, it is almost impossible to help you direct your study efforts. What we can do is to point out some of the more common of these general abilities needed in public service positions and describe some typical questions.

1) General information

Broad, general information has been found useful for predicting job success in some kinds of work. This is tested in a variety of ways, from vocabulary lists to questions about current events. Basic background in some field of work, such as sociology or economics, may be sampled in a group of questions. Often these are principles which have become familiar to most persons through exposure rather than through formal training. It is difficult to advise you how to study for these questions; being alert to the world around you is our best suggestion.

2) Verbal ability

An example of an ability needed in many positions is verbal or language ability. Verbal ability is, in brief, the ability to use and understand words. Vocabulary and grammar tests are typical measures of this ability. Reading comprehension or paragraph interpretation questions are common in many kinds of civil service tests. You are given a paragraph of written material and asked to find its central meaning.

3) Numerical ability

Number skills can be tested by the familiar arithmetic problem, by checking paired lists of numbers to see which are alike and which are different, or by interpreting charts and graphs. In the latter test, a graph may be printed in the test booklet which you are asked to use as the basis for answering questions.

4) Observation

A popular test for law-enforcement positions is the observation test. A picture is shown to you for several minutes, then taken away. Questions about the picture test your ability to observe both details and larger elements.

5) Following directions

In many positions in the public service, the employee must be able to carry out written instructions dependably and accurately. You may be given a chart with several columns, each column listing a variety of information. The questions require you to carry out directions involving the information given in the chart.

6) Skills and aptitudes

Performance tests effectively measure some manual skills and aptitudes. When the skill is one in which you are trained, such as typing or shorthand, you can practice. These tests are often very much like those given in business school or high school courses. For many of the other skills and aptitudes, however, no short-time preparation can be made. Skills and abilities natural to you or that you have developed throughout your lifetime are being tested.

Many of the general questions just described provide all the data needed to answer the questions and ask you to use your reasoning ability to find the answers. Your best preparation for these tests, as well as for tests of facts and ideas, is to be at your physical and mental best. You, no doubt, have your own methods of getting into an exam-taking mood and keeping "in shape." The next section lists some ideas on this subject.

IV. KINDS OF QUESTIONS

Only rarely is the "essay" question, which you answer in narrative form, used in civil service tests. Civil service tests are usually of the short-answer type. Full instructions for answering these questions will be given to you at the examination. But in case this is your first experience with short-answer questions and separate answer sheets, here is what you need to know:

1) Multiple-choice Questions

Most popular of the short-answer questions is the "multiple choice" or "best answer" question. It can be used, for example, to test for factual knowledge, ability to solve problems or judgment in meeting situations found at work.

A multiple-choice question is normally one of three types—
- It can begin with an incomplete statement followed by several possible endings. You are to find the one ending which *best* completes the statement, although some of the others may not be entirely wrong.
- It can also be a complete statement in the form of a question which is answered by choosing one of the statements listed.

- It can be in the form of a problem – again you select the best answer.

Here is an example of a multiple-choice question with a discussion which should give you some clues as to the method for choosing the right answer:

When an employee has a complaint about his assignment, the action which will *best* help him overcome his difficulty is to
  A. discuss his difficulty with his coworkers
  B. take the problem to the head of the organization
  C. take the problem to the person who gave him the assignment
  D. say nothing to anyone about his complaint

In answering this question, you should study each of the choices to find which is best. Consider choice "A" – Certainly an employee may discuss his complaint with fellow employees, but no change or improvement can result, and the complaint remains unresolved. Choice "B" is a poor choice since the head of the organization probably does not know what assignment you have been given, and taking your problem to him is known as "going over the head" of the supervisor. The supervisor, or person who made the assignment, is the person who can clarify it or correct any injustice. Choice "C" is, therefore, correct. To say nothing, as in choice "D," is unwise. Supervisors have and interest in knowing the problems employees are facing, and the employee is seeking a solution to his problem.

2) True/False Questions

The "true/false" or "right/wrong" form of question is sometimes used. Here a complete statement is given. Your job is to decide whether the statement is right or wrong.

SAMPLE: A roaming cell-phone call to a nearby city costs less than a non-roaming call to a distant city.

This statement is wrong, or false, since roaming calls are more expensive.
This is not a complete list of all possible question forms, although most of the others are variations of these common types. You will always get complete directions for answering questions. Be sure you understand *how* to mark your answers – ask questions until you do.

V. RECORDING YOUR ANSWERS

Computer terminals are used more and more today for many different kinds of exams.
For an examination with very few applicants, you may be told to record your answers in the test booklet itself. Separate answer sheets are much more common. If this separate answer sheet is to be scored by machine – and this is often the case – it is highly important that you mark your answers correctly in order to get credit.
An electronic scoring machine is often used in civil service offices because of the speed with which papers can be scored. Machine-scored answer sheets must be marked with a pencil, which will be given to you. This pencil has a high graphite content which responds to the electronic scoring machine. As a matter of fact, stray dots may register as answers, so do not let your pencil rest on the answer sheet while you are pondering the correct answer. Also, if your pencil lead breaks or is otherwise defective, ask for another.

Since the answer sheet will be dropped in a slot in the scoring machine, be careful not to bend the corners or get the paper crumpled.

The answer sheet normally has five vertical columns of numbers, with 30 numbers to a column. These numbers correspond to the question numbers in your test booklet. After each number, going across the page are four or five pairs of dotted lines. These short dotted lines have small letters or numbers above them. The first two pairs may also have a "T" or "F" above the letters. This indicates that the first two pairs only are to be used if the questions are of the true-false type. If the questions are multiple choice, disregard the "T" and "F" and pay attention only to the small letters or numbers.

Answer your questions in the manner of the sample that follows:

32. The largest city in the United States is
    A. Washington, D.C.
    B. New York City
    C. Chicago
    D. Detroit
    E. San Francisco

1) Choose the answer you think is best. (New York City is the largest, so "B" is correct.)
2) Find the row of dotted lines numbered the same as the question you are answering. (Find row number 32)
3) Find the pair of dotted lines corresponding to the answer. (Find the pair of lines under the mark "B.")
4) Make a solid black mark between the dotted lines.

VI. BEFORE THE TEST

Common sense will help you find procedures to follow to get ready for an examination. Too many of us, however, overlook these sensible measures. Indeed, nervousness and fatigue have been found to be the most serious reasons why applicants fail to do their best on civil service tests. Here is a list of reminders:

- Begin your preparation early – Don't wait until the last minute to go scurrying around for books and materials or to find out what the position is all about.
- Prepare continuously – An hour a night for a week is better than an all-night cram session. This has been definitely established. What is more, a night a week for a month will return better dividends than crowding your study into a shorter period of time.
- Locate the place of the exam – You have been sent a notice telling you when and where to report for the examination. If the location is in a different town or otherwise unfamiliar to you, it would be well to inquire the best route and learn something about the building.
- Relax the night before the test – Allow your mind to rest. Do not study at all that night. Plan some mild recreation or diversion; then go to bed early and get a good night's sleep.
- Get up early enough to make a leisurely trip to the place for the test – This way unforeseen events, traffic snarls, unfamiliar buildings, etc. will not upset you.
- Dress comfortably – A written test is not a fashion show. You will be known by number and not by name, so wear something comfortable.

- Leave excess paraphernalia at home – Shopping bags and odd bundles will get in your way. You need bring only the items mentioned in the official notice you received; usually everything you need is provided. Do not bring reference books to the exam. They will only confuse those last minutes and be taken away from you when in the test room.
- Arrive somewhat ahead of time – If because of transportation schedules you must get there very early, bring a newspaper or magazine to take your mind off yourself while waiting.
- Locate the examination room – When you have found the proper room, you will be directed to the seat or part of the room where you will sit. Sometimes you are given a sheet of instructions to read while you are waiting. Do not fill out any forms until you are told to do so; just read them and be prepared.
- Relax and prepare to listen to the instructions
- If you have any physical problem that may keep you from doing your best, be sure to tell the test administrator. If you are sick or in poor health, you really cannot do your best on the exam. You can come back and take the test some other time.

VII. AT THE TEST

The day of the test is here and you have the test booklet in your hand. The temptation to get going is very strong. Caution! There is more to success than knowing the right answers. You must know how to identify your papers and understand variations in the type of short-answer question used in this particular examination. Follow these suggestions for maximum results from your efforts:

1) Cooperate with the monitor

The test administrator has a duty to create a situation in which you can be as much at ease as possible. He will give instructions, tell you when to begin, check to see that you are marking your answer sheet correctly, and so on. He is not there to guard you, although he will see that your competitors do not take unfair advantage. He wants to help you do your best.

2) Listen to all instructions

Don't jump the gun! Wait until you understand all directions. In most civil service tests you get more time than you need to answer the questions. So don't be in a hurry. Read each word of instructions until you clearly understand the meaning. Study the examples, listen to all announcements and follow directions. Ask questions if you do not understand what to do.

3) Identify your papers

Civil service exams are usually identified by number only. You will be assigned a number; you must not put your name on your test papers. Be sure to copy your number correctly. Since more than one exam may be given, copy your exact examination title.

4) Plan your time

Unless you are told that a test is a "speed" or "rate of work" test, speed itself is usually not important. Time enough to answer all the questions will be provided, but this does not mean that you have all day. An overall time limit has been set. Divide the total time (in minutes) by the number of questions to determine the approximate time you have for each question.

5) Do not linger over difficult questions

If you come across a difficult question, mark it with a paper clip (useful to have along) and come back to it when you have been through the booklet. One caution if you do this – be sure to skip a number on your answer sheet as well. Check often to be sure that you have not lost your place and that you are marking in the row numbered the same as the question you are answering.

6) Read the questions

Be sure you know what the question asks! Many capable people are unsuccessful because they failed to *read* the questions correctly.

7) Answer all questions

Unless you have been instructed that a penalty will be deducted for incorrect answers, it is better to guess than to omit a question.

8) Speed tests

It is often better NOT to guess on speed tests. It has been found that on timed tests people are tempted to spend the last few seconds before time is called in marking answers at random – without even reading them – in the hope of picking up a few extra points. To discourage this practice, the instructions may warn you that your score will be "corrected" for guessing. That is, a penalty will be applied. The incorrect answers will be deducted from the correct ones, or some other penalty formula will be used.

9) Review your answers

If you finish before time is called, go back to the questions you guessed or omitted to give them further thought. Review other answers if you have time.

10) Return your test materials

If you are ready to leave before others have finished or time is called, take ALL your materials to the monitor and leave quietly. Never take any test material with you. The monitor can discover whose papers are not complete, and taking a test booklet may be grounds for disqualification.

VIII. EXAMINATION TECHNIQUES

1) Read the general instructions carefully. These are usually printed on the first page of the exam booklet. As a rule, these instructions refer to the timing of the examination; the fact that you should not start work until the signal and must stop work at a signal, etc. If there are any *special* instructions, such as a choice of questions to be answered, make sure that you note this instruction carefully.

2) When you are ready to start work on the examination, that is as soon as the signal has been given, read the instructions to each question booklet, underline any key words or phrases, such as *least, best, outline, describe* and the like. In this way you will tend to answer as requested rather than discover on reviewing your paper that you *listed without describing*, that you selected the *worst* choice rather than the *best* choice, etc.

3) If the examination is of the objective or multiple-choice type – that is, each question will also give a series of possible answers: A, B, C or D, and you are called upon to select the best answer and write the letter next to that answer on your answer paper – it is advisable to start answering each question in turn. There may be anywhere from 50 to 100 such questions in the three or four hours allotted and you can see how much time would be taken if you read through all the questions before beginning to answer any. Furthermore, if you come across a question or group of questions which you know would be difficult to answer, it would undoubtedly affect your handling of all the other questions.

4) If the examination is of the essay type and contains but a few questions, it is a moot point as to whether you should read all the questions before starting to answer any one. Of course, if you are given a choice – say five out of seven and the like – then it is essential to read all the questions so you can eliminate the two that are most difficult. If, however, you are asked to answer all the questions, there may be danger in trying to answer the easiest one first because you may find that you will spend too much time on it. The best technique is to answer the first question, then proceed to the second, etc.

5) Time your answers. Before the exam begins, write down the time it started, then add the time allowed for the examination and write down the time it must be completed, then divide the time available somewhat as follows:
    - If 3-1/2 hours are allowed, that would be 210 minutes. If you have 80 objective-type questions, that would be an average of 2-1/2 minutes per question. Allow yourself no more than 2 minutes per question, or a total of 160 minutes, which will permit about 50 minutes to review.
    - If for the time allotment of 210 minutes there are 7 essay questions to answer, that would average about 30 minutes a question. Give yourself only 25 minutes per question so that you have about 35 minutes to review.

6) The most important instruction is to *read each question* and make sure you know what is wanted. The second most important instruction is to *time yourself properly* so that you answer every question. The third most important instruction is to *answer every question*. Guess if you have to but include something for each question. Remember that you will receive no credit for a blank and will probably receive some credit if you write something in answer to an essay question. If you guess a letter – say "B" for a multiple-choice question – you may have guessed right. If you leave a blank as an answer to a multiple-choice question, the examiners may respect your feelings but it will not add a point to your score. Some exams may penalize you for wrong answers, so in such cases *only*, you may not want to guess unless you have some basis for your answer.

7) Suggestions
    a. Objective-type questions
        1. Examine the question booklet for proper sequence of pages and questions
        2. Read all instructions carefully
        3. Skip any question which seems too difficult; return to it after all other questions have been answered
        4. Apportion your time properly; do not spend too much time on any single question or group of questions

5. Note and underline key words – *all, most, fewest, least, best, worst, same, opposite,* etc.
6. Pay particular attention to negatives
7. Note unusual option, e.g., unduly long, short, complex, different or similar in content to the body of the question
8. Observe the use of "hedging" words – *probably, may, most likely,* etc.
9. Make sure that your answer is put next to the same number as the question
10. Do not second-guess unless you have good reason to believe the second answer is definitely more correct
11. Cross out original answer if you decide another answer is more accurate; do not erase until you are ready to hand your paper in
12. Answer all questions; guess unless instructed otherwise
13. Leave time for review

b. Essay questions
1. Read each question carefully
2. Determine exactly what is wanted. Underline key words or phrases.
3. Decide on outline or paragraph answer
4. Include many different points and elements unless asked to develop any one or two points or elements
5. Show impartiality by giving pros and cons unless directed to select one side only
6. Make and write down any assumptions you find necessary to answer the questions
7. Watch your English, grammar, punctuation and choice of words
8. Time your answers; don't crowd material

8) Answering the essay question

Most essay questions can be answered by framing the specific response around several key words or ideas. Here are a few such key words or ideas:

M's: manpower, materials, methods, money, management
P's: purpose, program, policy, plan, procedure, practice, problems, pitfalls, personnel, public relations

a. Six basic steps in handling problems:
1. Preliminary plan and background development
2. Collect information, data and facts
3. Analyze and interpret information, data and facts
4. Analyze and develop solutions as well as make recommendations
5. Prepare report and sell recommendations
6. Install recommendations and follow up effectiveness

b. Pitfalls to avoid
1. *Taking things for granted* – A statement of the situation does not necessarily imply that each of the elements is necessarily true; for example, a complaint may be invalid and biased so that all that can be taken for granted is that a complaint has been registered

2. *Considering only one side of a situation* – Wherever possible, indicate several alternatives and then point out the reasons you selected the best one
3. *Failing to indicate follow up* – Whenever your answer indicates action on your part, make certain that you will take proper follow-up action to see how successful your recommendations, procedures or actions turn out to be
4. *Taking too long in answering any single question* – Remember to time your answers properly

IX. AFTER THE TEST

Scoring procedures differ in detail among civil service jurisdictions although the general principles are the same. Whether the papers are hand-scored or graded by machine we have described, they are nearly always graded by number. That is, the person who marks the paper knows only the number – never the name – of the applicant. Not until all the papers have been graded will they be matched with names. If other tests, such as training and experience or oral interview ratings have been given, scores will be combined. Different parts of the examination usually have different weights. For example, the written test might count 60 percent of the final grade, and a rating of training and experience 40 percent. In many jurisdictions, veterans will have a certain number of points added to their grades.

After the final grade has been determined, the names are placed in grade order and an eligible list is established. There are various methods for resolving ties between those who get the same final grade – probably the most common is to place first the name of the person whose application was received first. Job offers are made from the eligible list in the order the names appear on it. You will be notified of your grade and your rank as soon as all these computations have been made. This will be done as rapidly as possible.

People who are found to meet the requirements in the announcement are called "eligibles." Their names are put on a list of eligible candidates. An eligible's chances of getting a job depend on how high he stands on this list and how fast agencies are filling jobs from the list.

When a job is to be filled from a list of eligibles, the agency asks for the names of people on the list of eligibles for that job. When the civil service commission receives this request, it sends to the agency the names of the three people highest on this list. Or, if the job to be filled has specialized requirements, the office sends the agency the names of the top three persons who meet these requirements from the general list.

The appointing officer makes a choice from among the three people whose names were sent to him. If the selected person accepts the appointment, the names of the others are put back on the list to be considered for future openings.

That is the rule in hiring from all kinds of eligible lists, whether they are for typist, carpenter, chemist, or something else. For every vacancy, the appointing officer has his choice of any one of the top three eligibles on the list. This explains why the person whose name is on top of the list sometimes does not get an appointment when some of the persons lower on the list do. If the appointing officer chooses the second or third eligible, the No. 1 eligible does not get a job at once, but stays on the list until he is appointed or the list is terminated.

X. HOW TO PASS THE INTERVIEW TEST

The examination for which you applied requires an oral interview test. You have already taken the written test and you are now being called for the interview test – the final part of the formal examination.

You may think that it is not possible to prepare for an interview test and that there are no procedures to follow during an interview. Our purpose is to point out some things you can do in advance that will help you and some good rules to follow and pitfalls to avoid while you are being interviewed.

What is an interview supposed to test?

The written examination is designed to test the technical knowledge and competence of the candidate; the oral is designed to evaluate intangible qualities, not readily measured otherwise, and to establish a list showing the relative fitness of each candidate – as measured against his competitors – for the position sought. Scoring is not on the basis of "right" and "wrong," but on a sliding scale of values ranging from "not passable" to "outstanding." As a matter of fact, it is possible to achieve a relatively low score without a single "incorrect" answer because of evident weakness in the qualities being measured.

Occasionally, an examination may consist entirely of an oral test – either an individual or a group oral. In such cases, information is sought concerning the technical knowledges and abilities of the candidate, since there has been no written examination for this purpose. More commonly, however, an oral test is used to supplement a written examination.

Who conducts interviews?

The composition of oral boards varies among different jurisdictions. In nearly all, a representative of the personnel department serves as chairman. One of the members of the board may be a representative of the department in which the candidate would work. In some cases, "outside experts" are used, and, frequently, a businessman or some other representative of the general public is asked to serve. Labor and management or other special groups may be represented. The aim is to secure the services of experts in the appropriate field.

However the board is composed, it is a good idea (and not at all improper or unethical) to ascertain in advance of the interview who the members are and what groups they represent. When you are introduced to them, you will have some idea of their backgrounds and interests, and at least you will not stutter and stammer over their names.

What should be done before the interview?

While knowledge about the board members is useful and takes some of the surprise element out of the interview, there is other preparation which is more substantive. It *is* possible to prepare for an oral interview – in several ways:

1) Keep a copy of your application and review it carefully before the interview

This may be the only document before the oral board, and the starting point of the interview. Know what education and experience you have listed there, and the sequence and dates of all of it. Sometimes the board will ask you to review the highlights of your experience for them; you should not have to hem and haw doing it.

2) Study the class specification and the examination announcement

Usually, the oral board has one or both of these to guide them. The qualities, characteristics or knowledges required by the position sought are stated in these documents. They offer valuable clues as to the nature of the oral interview. For example, if the job involves supervisory responsibilities, the announcement will usually indicate that knowledge of modern supervisory methods and the qualifications of the candidate as a supervisor will be tested. If so, you can expect such questions, frequently in the form of a hypothetical situation which you are expected to solve. NEVER go into an oral without knowledge of the duties and responsibilities of the job you seek.

3) Think through each qualification required

Try to visualize the kind of questions you would ask if you were a board member. How well could you answer them? Try especially to appraise your own knowledge and background in each area, *measured against the job sought*, and identify any areas in which you are weak. Be critical and realistic – do not flatter yourself.

4) Do some general reading in areas in which you feel you may be weak

For example, if the job involves supervision and your past experience has NOT, some general reading in supervisory methods and practices, particularly in the field of human relations, might be useful. Do NOT study agency procedures or detailed manuals. The oral board will be testing your understanding and capacity, not your memory.

5) Get a good night's sleep and watch your general health and mental attitude

You will want a clear head at the interview. Take care of a cold or any other minor ailment, and of course, no hangovers.

What should be done on the day of the interview?

Now comes the day of the interview itself. Give yourself plenty of time to get there. Plan to arrive somewhat ahead of the scheduled time, particularly if your appointment is in the fore part of the day. If a previous candidate fails to appear, the board might be ready for you a bit early. By early afternoon an oral board is almost invariably behind schedule if there are many candidates, and you may have to wait. Take along a book or magazine to read, or your application to review, but leave any extraneous material in the waiting room when you go in for your interview. In any event, relax and compose yourself.

The matter of dress is important. The board is forming impressions about you – from your experience, your manners, your attitude, and your appearance. Give your personal appearance careful attention. Dress your best, but not your flashiest. Choose conservative, appropriate clothing, and be sure it is immaculate. This is a business interview, and your appearance should indicate that you regard it as such. Besides, being well groomed and properly dressed will help boost your confidence.

Sooner or later, someone will call your name and escort you into the interview room. *This is it.* From here on you are on your own. It is too late for any more preparation. But remember, you asked for this opportunity to prove your fitness, and you are here because your request was granted.

What happens when you go in?

The usual sequence of events will be as follows: The clerk (who is often the board stenographer) will introduce you to the chairman of the oral board, who will introduce you to the other members of the board. Acknowledge the introductions before you sit down. Do not be surprised if you find a microphone facing you or a stenotypist sitting by. Oral interviews are usually recorded in the event of an appeal or other review.

Usually the chairman of the board will open the interview by reviewing the highlights of your education and work experience from your application – primarily for the benefit of the other members of the board, as well as to get the material into the record. Do not interrupt or comment unless there is an error or significant misinterpretation; if that is the case, do not hesitate. But do not quibble about insignificant matters. Also, he will usually ask you some question about your education, experience or your present job – partly to get you to start talking and to establish the interviewing "rapport." He may start the actual questioning, or turn it over to one of the other members. Frequently, each member undertakes the questioning on a particular area, one in which he is perhaps most competent, so you can expect each member to participate in the examination. Because time is limited, you may also expect some rather abrupt switches in the direction the questioning takes, so do not be upset by it. Normally, a board member will not pursue a single line of questioning unless he discovers a particular strength or weakness.

After each member has participated, the chairman will usually ask whether any member has any further questions, then will ask you if you have anything you wish to add. Unless you are expecting this question, it may floor you. Worse, it may start you off on an extended, extemporaneous speech. The board is not usually seeking more information. The question is principally to offer you a last opportunity to present further qualifications or to indicate that you have nothing to add. So, if you feel that a significant qualification or characteristic has been overlooked, it is proper to point it out in a sentence or so. Do not compliment the board on the thoroughness of their examination – they have been sketchy, and you know it. If you wish, merely say, "No thank you, I have nothing further to add." This is a point where you can "talk yourself out" of a good impression or fail to present an important bit of information. Remember, *you close the interview yourself.*

The chairman will then say, "That is all, Mr. _____, thank you." Do not be startled; the interview is over, and quicker than you think. Thank him, gather your belongings and take your leave. Save your sigh of relief for the other side of the door.

How to put your best foot forward

Throughout this entire process, you may feel that the board individually and collectively is trying to pierce your defenses, seek out your hidden weaknesses and embarrass and confuse you. Actually, this is not true. They are obliged to make an appraisal of your qualifications for the job you are seeking, and they want to see you in your best light. Remember, they must interview all candidates and a non-cooperative candidate may become a failure in spite of their best efforts to bring out his qualifications. Here are 15 suggestions that will help you:

1) Be natural – Keep your attitude confident, not cocky

If you are not confident that you can do the job, do not expect the board to be. Do not apologize for your weaknesses, try to bring out your strong points. The board is interested in a positive, not negative, presentation. Cockiness will antagonize any board member and make him wonder if you are covering up a weakness by a false show of strength.

2) Get comfortable, but don't lounge or sprawl

Sit erectly but not stiffly. A careless posture may lead the board to conclude that you are careless in other things, or at least that you are not impressed by the importance of the occasion. Either conclusion is natural, even if incorrect. Do not fuss with your clothing, a pencil or an ashtray. Your hands may occasionally be useful to emphasize a point; do not let them become a point of distraction.

3) Do not wisecrack or make small talk

This is a serious situation, and your attitude should show that you consider it as such. Further, the time of the board is limited – they do not want to waste it, and neither should you.

4) Do not exaggerate your experience or abilities

In the first place, from information in the application or other interviews and sources, the board may know more about you than you think. Secondly, you probably will not get away with it. An experienced board is rather adept at spotting such a situation, so do not take the chance.

5) If you know a board member, do not make a point of it, yet do not hide it

Certainly you are not fooling him, and probably not the other members of the board. Do not try to take advantage of your acquaintanceship – it will probably do you little good.

6) Do not dominate the interview

Let the board do that. They will give you the clues – do not assume that you have to do all the talking. Realize that the board has a number of questions to ask you, and do not try to take up all the interview time by showing off your extensive knowledge of the answer to the first one.

7) Be attentive

You only have 20 minutes or so, and you should keep your attention at its sharpest throughout. When a member is addressing a problem or question to you, give him your undivided attention. Address your reply principally to him, but do not exclude the other board members.

8) Do not interrupt

A board member may be stating a problem for you to analyze. He will ask you a question when the time comes. Let him state the problem, and wait for the question.

9) Make sure you understand the question

Do not try to answer until you are sure what the question is. If it is not clear, restate it in your own words or ask the board member to clarify it for you. However, do not haggle about minor elements.

10) Reply promptly but not hastily

A common entry on oral board rating sheets is "candidate responded readily," or "candidate hesitated in replies." Respond as promptly and quickly as you can, but do not jump to a hasty, ill-considered answer.

11) Do not be peremptory in your answers

A brief answer is proper – but do not fire your answer back. That is a losing game from your point of view. The board member can probably ask questions much faster than you can answer them.

12) Do not try to create the answer you think the board member wants

He is interested in what kind of mind you have and how it works – not in playing games. Furthermore, he can usually spot this practice and will actually grade you down on it.

13) Do not switch sides in your reply merely to agree with a board member

Frequently, a member will take a contrary position merely to draw you out and to see if you are willing and able to defend your point of view. Do not start a debate, yet do not surrender a good position. If a position is worth taking, it is worth defending.

14) Do not be afraid to admit an error in judgment if you are shown to be wrong

The board knows that you are forced to reply without any opportunity for careful consideration. Your answer may be demonstrably wrong. If so, admit it and get on with the interview.

15) Do not dwell at length on your present job

The opening question may relate to your present assignment. Answer the question but do not go into an extended discussion. You are being examined for a *new* job, not your present one. As a matter of fact, try to phrase ALL your answers in terms of the job for which you are being examined.

Basis of Rating

Probably you will forget most of these "do's" and "don'ts" when you walk into the oral interview room. Even remembering them all will not ensure you a passing grade. Perhaps you did not have the qualifications in the first place. But remembering them will help you to put your best foot forward, without treading on the toes of the board members.

Rumor and popular opinion to the contrary notwithstanding, an oral board wants you to make the best appearance possible. They know you are under pressure – but they also want to see how you respond to it as a guide to what your reaction would be under the pressures of the job you seek. They will be influenced by the degree of poise you display, the personal traits you show and the manner in which you respond.

ABOUT THIS BOOK

This book contains tests divided into Examination Sections. Go through each test, answering every question in the margin. We have also attached a sample answer sheet at the back of the book that can be removed and used. At the end of each test look at the answer key and check your answers. On the ones you got wrong, look at the right answer choice and learn. Do not fill in the answers first. Do not memorize the questions and answers, but understand the answer and principles involved. On your test, the questions will likely be different from the samples. Questions are changed and new ones added. If you understand these past questions you should have success with any changes that arise. Tests may consist of several types of questions. We have additional books on each subject should more study be advisable or necessary for you. Finally, the more you study, the better prepared you will be. This book is intended to be the last thing you study before you walk into the examination room. Prior study of relevant texts is also recommended. NLC publishes some of these in our Fundamental Series. Knowledge and good sense are important factors in passing your exam. Good luck also helps. So now study this Passbook, absorb the material contained within and take that knowledge into the examination. Then do your best to pass that exam.

EXAMINATION SECTION

EXAMINATION SECTION
TEST 1

DIRECTIONS: Each question or incomplete statement is followed by several suggested answers or completions. Select the one that BEST answers the question or completes the statement. *PRINT THE LETTER OF THE CORRECT ANSWER IN THE SPACE AT THE RIGHT.*

1. The officer who investigates accidents is always required to make a complete and accurate report.
   Of the following, the BEST reason for this procedure is to

   A. protect the operating agency against possible false claims
   B. provide a file of incidents which can be used as basic material for an accident prevention campaign
   C. provide the management with concrete evidence of violations of the rules by employees
   D. indicate what repairs need to be made

   1.____

2. It is suggested that an officer keep all persons away from the area of an accident until an investigation has been completed.
   This suggested procedure is

   A. *good;* witnesses will be more likely to agree on a single story
   B. *bad;* such action blocks traffic flow and causes congestion
   C. *good;* objects of possible use as evidence will be protected from damage or loss
   D. *bad;* the flow of normal pedestrian traffic provides an opportunity for an investigator to determine the cause of the accident

   2.____

3. A man having business with your agency is arguing with you and accuses you of being prejudiced against him. Although you explain to him that this is not so, he demands to see your supervisor.
   Of the following, the BEST course of action for you to take is to

   A. continue arguing with him until you have worn him out or convinced him
   B. take him to your supervisor
   C. ignore him and walk away from him to another part of the office
   D. escort him out of the office

   3.____

4. An officer receives instructions from his supervisor which he does not fully understand.
   For the officer to ask for a further explanation would be

   A. *good;* chiefly because his supervisor will be impressed with his interest in his work
   B. *poor;* chiefly because the time of the supervisor will be needlessly wasted
   C. *good;* chiefly because proper performance depends on full understanding of the work to be done
   D. *poor;* chiefly because officers should be able to think for themselves

   4.____

5. A person is making a complaint to an officer which seems unreasonable and of little importance.
   Of the following, the BEST action for the officer to take is to

   5.____

A. criticize the person making the complaint for taking up his valuable time
B. laugh over the matter to show that the complaint is minor and silly
C. tell the person that anyone responsible for his grievance will be prosecuted
D. listen to the person making the complaint and tell him that the matter will be investigated

6. A member of the department shall not indulge in intoxicating liquor while in uniform. A member of the department is not required to wear a uniform, and a uniformed member while out of uniform shall not indulge in intoxicants to an extent unfitting him for duty. Of the following, the MOST correct interpretation of this rule is that a 6.____

   A. member, off duty, not in uniform, may drink intoxicating liquor
   B. member, not on duty, but in uniform, may drink intoxicating liquor
   C. member, on duty, in uniform, may drink intoxicants
   D. uniformed member, in civilian clothes, may not drink intoxicants

7. You have a suggestion for an important change which you believe will improve a certain procedure in your agency. Of the following, the next course of action for you to take is to 7.____

   A. try it out yourself
   B. submit the suggestion to your immediate supervisor
   C. write a letter to the head of your agency asking for his approval
   D. wait until you are asked for suggestions before submitting this one

8. An officer shall study maps and literature concerning his assigned area and the streets and points of interest nearby. 8.____
   Of the following, the BEST reason for this rule is that

   A. the officer will be better able to give correct information to persons desiring it
   B. the officer will be better able to drive a vehicle in the area
   C. the officer will not lose interest in his work
   D. supervisors will not need to train the officers in this subject

9. In asking a witness to a crime to identify a suspect, it is a common practice to place the suspect with a group of persons and ask the witness to pick out the person in question. 9.____
   Of the following, the BEST reason for this practice is that it will

   A. make the identification more reliable than if the witness were shown the suspect alone
   B. protect the witness against reprisals
   C. make sure that the witness is telling the truth
   D. help select other participants in the crime at the same time

10. It is most important for all officers to obey the "Rules and Regulations" of their agency. 10.____
    Of the following, the BEST reason for this statement is that

    A. supervisors will not need to train their new officers
    B. officers will never have to use their own judgment
    C. uniform procedures will be followed
    D. officers will not need to ask their supervisors for assistance

Questions 11-13.

DIRECTIONS: Answer questions 11 to 13 SOLELY on the basis of the following paragraph.

All members of the police force must recognize that the people, through their representatives, hire and pay the police and that, as in any other employment, there must exist a proper employer-employee relationship. The police officer must understand that the essence of a correct police attitude is a willingness to serve, but at the same time, he should distinguish between service and servility, and between courtesy and softness. He must be firm but also courteous, avoiding even an appearance of rudeness. He should develop a position that is friendly and unbiased, pleasant and sympathetic, in his relations with the general public, but firm and impersonal on occasions calling for regulation and control. A police officer should understand that his primary purpose is to prevent violations, not to arrest people. He should recognize the line of demarcation between a police function and passing judgment which is a court function. On the other side, a public that cooperates with the police, that supports them in their efforts and that observes laws and regulations, may be said to have a desirable attitude.

11. In accordance with this paragraph, the PROPER attitude for a police officer to take is to   11._____

    A. be pleasant and sympathetic at all times
    B. be friendly, firm, and impartial
    C. be stern and severe in meting out justice to all
    D. avoid being rude, except in those cases where the public is uncooperative

12. Assume that an officer is assigned by his superior officer to a busy traffic intersection and   12._____
    is warned to be on the lookout for motorists who skip the light or who are speeding.
    According to this paragraph, it would be proper for the officer in this assignment to

    A. give a summons to every motorist whose ear was crossing when the light changed
    B. hide behind a truck and wait for drivers who violate traffic laws
    C. select at random motorists who seem to be impatient and lecture them sternly on traffic safety
    D. stand on post in order to deter violations and give offenders a summons or a warning as required

13. According to this paragraph, a police officer must realize that the primary purpose of   13._____
    police work is to

    A. provide proper police service in a courteous manner
    B. decide whether those who violate the law should be punished
    C. arrest those who violate laws
    D. establish a proper employer-employee relationship

Questions 14-15.

DIRECTIONS: Answer questions 14 and 15 SOLELY on the basis of the following paragraph.

If a motor vehicle fails to pass inspection, the owner will be given a rejection notice by the inspection station. Repairs must be made within ten days after this notice is issued. It is not necessary to have the required adjustment or repairs made at the station where the inspection occurred. The vehicle may be taken to any other garage. Re-inspection after repairs may be made at any official inspection station, not necessarily the same station which made the initial inspection. The registration of any motor vehicle for which an inspection sticker has not been obtained as required, or which is not repaired and inspected within ten days after inspection indicates defects, is subject to suspension. A vehicle cannot be used on public highways while its registration is under suspension.

14. According to the above paragraph, the owner of a car which does NOT pass inspection must

    A. have repairs made at the same station which rejected his car
    B. take the car to another station and have it re-inspected
    C. have repairs made anywhere and then have the car re-inspected
    D. not use the car on a public highway until the necessary repairs have been made

15. According to the above paragraph, the one of the following which may be cause for suspension of the registration of a vehicle is that

    A. an inspection sticker was issued before the rejection notice had been in force for ten days
    B. it was not re-inspected by the station that rejected it originally
    C. it was not re-inspected either by the station that rejected it originally or by the garage which made the repairs
    D. it has not had defective parts repaired within ten days after inspection

Questions 16-20.

DIRECTIONS: Answer questions 16 to 20 SOLELY on the basis of the following paragraph.

If we are to study crime in its widest social setting, we will find a variety of conduct which, although criminal in the legal sense, is not offensive to the moral conscience of a considerable number of persons. Traffic violations, for example, do not brand the offender as guilty of moral offense. In fact, the recipient of a traffic ticket is usually simply the subject of some good-natured joking by his friends. Although there may be indignation among certain groups of citizens against gambling and liquor law violations, these activities are often tolerated, if not openly supported, by the more numerous residents of the community. Indeed, certain social and service clubs regularly conduct gambling games and lotteries for the purpose of raising funds. Some communities regard violations involving the sale of liquor with little concern in order to profit from increased license fees and taxes paid by dealers. The thousand and one forms of political graft and corruption which infest our urban centers only occasionally arouse public condemnation and official action.

16. According to the paragraph, all types of illegal conduct are

    A. condemned by all elements of the community
    B. considered a moral offense, although some are tolerated by a few citizens
    C. violations of the law, but some are acceptable to certain elements of the community
    D. found in a social setting which is not punishable by law

17. According to the paragraph, traffic violations are generally considered by society as

    A. crimes requiring the maximum penalty set by the law
    B. more serious than violations of the liquor laws

C. offenses against the morals of the community
D. relatively minor offenses requiring minimum punishment

18. According to the paragraph, a lottery conducted for the purpose of raising funds for a church

    A. is considered a serious violation of law
    B. may be tolerated by a community which has laws against gambling
    C. may be conducted under special laws demanded by the more numerous residents of a community
    D. arouses indignation in most communities

19. On the basis of the paragraph, the MOST likely reaction in the community to a police raid on a gambling casino would be

    A. more an attitude of indifference than interest in the raid
    B. general approval of the raid
    C. condemnation of the raid by most people
    D. demand for further action since this raid is not sufficient to end gambling activities

20. The one of the following which BEST describes the central thought of this paragraph and would be MOST suitable as a title for it is

    A. CRIME AND THE POLICE
    B. PUBLIC CONDEMNATION OF GRAFT AND CORRUPTION
    C. GAMBLING IS NOT ALWAYS A VICIOUS BUSINESS
    D. PUBLIC ATTITUDE TOWARD LAW VIOLATIONS

Questions 21-23.

DIRECTIONS: Answer questions 21 to 23 SOLELY on the basis of the following paragraph.

The law enforcement agency is one of the most important agencies in the field of juvenile delinquency prevention. This is so not because of the social work connected with this problem, however, for this is not a police matter, but because the officers are usually the first to come in contact with the delinquent. The manner of arrest and detention makes a deep impression upon him and affects his life-long attitude toward society and the law. The juvenile court is perhaps the most important agency in this work. Contrary to the general opinion, however, it is not primarily concerned with putting children into correctional schools. The main purpose of the juvenile court is to save the child and to develop his emotional make-up in order that he can grow up to be a decent and well-balanced citizen. The system of probation is the means whereby the court seeks to accomplish these goals.

21. According to this paragraph, police work is an important part of a program to prevent juvenile delinquency because

    A. social work is no longer considered important in juvenile delinquency prevention
    B. police officers are the first to have contact with the delinquent
    C. police officers jail the offender in order to be able to change his attitude toward society and the law
    D. it is the first step in placing the delinquent in jail

22. According to this paragraph, the CHIEF purpose of the juvenile court is to 22.____

    A. punish the child for his offense
    B. select a suitable correctional school for the delinquent
    C. use available means to help the delinquent become a better person
    D. provide psychiatric care for the delinquent

23. According to this paragraph, the juvenile court directs the development of delinquents 23.____
    under its care CHIEFLY by

    A. placing the child under probation
    B. sending the child to a correctional school
    C. keeping the delinquent in prison
    D. returning the child to his home

Questions 24-27.

DIRECTIONS: Answer questions 24 to 27 SOLELY on the basis of the following paragraph.

When a vehicle has been disabled in the tunnel, the officer on patrol in this zone shall press the EMERGENCY TRUCK light button. In the fast lane, red lights will go on throughout the tunnel; in the slow lane, amber lights will go on throughout the tunnel. The yellow zone light will go on at each signal control station throughout the tunnel and will flash the number of the zone in which the stoppage has occurred. A red flashing pilot light will appear only at the signal control station at which the EMERGENCY TRUCK button was pressed. The emergency garage will receive an audible and visual signal indicating the signal control station at which the EMERGENCY TRUCK button was pressed. The garage officer shall acknowledge receipt of the signal by pressing the acknowledgment button. This will cause the pilot light at the operated signal control station in the tunnel to cease flashing and to remain steady. It is an answer to the officer at the operated signal control station that the emergency truck is responding to the call.

24. According to this paragraph, when the EMERGENCY TRUCK light button is pressed, 24.____

    A. amber lights will go on in every lane throughout the tunnel
    B. emergency signal lights will go on only in the lane in which the disabled vehicle happens to be
    C. red lights will go on in the fast lane throughout the tunnel
    D. pilot lights at all signal control stations will turn amber

25. According to this paragraph, the number of the zone in which the stoppage has occurred 25.____
    is flashed

    A. immediately after all the lights in the tunnel turn red
    B. by the yellow zone light at each signal control station
    C. by the emergency truck at the point of stoppage
    D. by the emergency garage

26. According to this paragraph, an officer near the disabled vehicle will know that the emer- 26.____
    gency tow truck is coming when

    A. the pilot light at the operated signal control station appears and flashes red
    B. an audible signal is heard in the tunnel

C. the zone light at the operated signal control station turns red
D. the pilot light at the operated signal control station becomes steady

27. Under the system described in the paragraph, it would be CORRECT to come to the conclusion that   27._____

   A. officers at all signal control stations are expected to acknowledge that they have received the stoppage signal
   B. officers at all signal control stations will know where the stoppage has occurred
   C. all traffic in both lanes of that side of the tunnel in which the stoppage has occurred must stop until the emergency truck has arrived
   D. there are two emergency garages, each able to respond to stoppages in traffic going in one particular direction

Questions 28-30.

DIRECTIONS: Answer questions 28 to 30 SOLELY on the basis of the following paragraphs.

In cases of accident, it is most important for an officer to obtain the name, age, residence, occupation, and a full description of the person injured, names and addresses of witnesses. He shall also obtain a statement of the attendant circumstances. He shall carefully note contributory conditions, if any, such as broken pavement, excavation, tights not burning, snow and ice on the roadway, etc. He shall enter all facts in his memorandum book and on Form 17 or Form 18 and promptly transmit the original of the form to his superior officer and the duplicate to headquarters.

An officer shall render reasonable assistance to sick or injured persons. If the circumstances appear to require the services of a physician, he shall summon a physician by telephoning the superior officer on duty and notifying him of the apparent nature of the illness or accident and the location where the physician will be required. He may summon other officers to assist if circumstances warrant.

In case of an accident or where a person is sick on city property, an officer shall obtain the information necessary to fill out card Form 18 and record this in his memorandum book and promptly telephone the facts to his superior officer. He shall deliver the original card at the expiration of his tour to his superior officer and transmit the duplicate to headquarters.

28. According to this quotation, the MOST important consideration in any report on a case of accident or injury is to   28._____

   A. obtain all the facts
   B. telephone his superior officer at once
   C. obtain a statement of the attendant circumstances
   D. determine ownership of the property on which the accident occurred

29. According to this quotation, in the case of an accident on city property, the officer should always   29._____

   A. summon a physician before filling out any forms or making any entries in his memorandum book
   B. give his superior officer on duty a prompt report by telephone

C. immediately bring the original of Form 18 to his superior officer on duty
D. call at least one other officer to the scene to witness conditions

30. If the procedures stated in this quotation were followed for all accidents in the city, an impartial survey of accidents occurring during any period of time in this city may be MOST easily made by

    A. asking a typical officer to show you his memorandum book
    B. having a superior officer investigate whether contributory conditions mentioned by witnesses actually exist
    C. checking all the records of all superior officers
    D. checking the duplicate card files at headquarters

Questions 31-55.

DIRECTIONS: In each of questions 31 to 55, select the lettered word or phrase which means MOST NEARLY the same as the first word in the row.

31. RENDEZVOUS

    A. parade   B. neighborhood
    C. meeting place   D. wander about

32. EMINENT

    A. noted   B. rich   C. rounded   D. nearby

33. CAUSTIC

    A. cheap   B. sweet   C. evil   D. sharp

34. BARTER

    A. annoy   B. trade   C. argue   D. cheat

35. APTITUDE

    A. friendliness   B. talent
    C. conceit   D. generosity

36. PROTRUDE

    A. project   B. defend   C. choke   D. boast

37. FORTITUDE

    A. disposition   B. restlessness
    C. courage   D. poverty

38. PRELUDE

    A. introduction   B. meaning
    C. prayer   D. secret

39. SECLUSION

    A. primitive   B. influence
    C. imagination D. privacy

40. RECTIFY 40.____
    A. correct   B. construct   C. divide   D. scold
41. TRAVERSE 41.____
    A. rotate   B. compose   C. train   D. cross
42. ALLEGE 42.____
    A. raise   B. convict   C. declare   D. chase
43. MENIAL 43.____
    A. pleasant   B. unselfish
    C. humble   D. stupid
44. DEPLETE 44.____
    A. exhaust   B. gather   C. repay   D. close
45. ERADICATE 45.____
    A. construct   B. advise   C. destroy   D. exclaim
46. CAPITULATE 46.____
    A. cover   B. surrender   C. receive   D. execute
47. RESTRAIN 47.____
    A. restore   B. drive   C. review   D. limit
48. AMALGAMATE 48.____
    A. join   B. force   C. correct   D. clash
49. DEJECTED 49.____
    A. beaten   B. speechless
    C. weak   D. low-spirited
50. DETAIN 50.____
    A. hide   B. accuse   C. hold   D. mislead

KEY (CORRECT ANSWERS)

1. A	11. B	21. B	31. C	41. D
2. C	12. D	22. C	32. A	42. C
3. B	13. A	23. A	33. D	43. C
4. C	14. C	24. C	34. B	44. A
5. D	15. D	25. B	35. B	45. C
6. A	16. C	26. D	36. A	46. B
7. B	17. D	27. B	37. C	47. D
8. A	18. B	28. A	38. A	48. A
9. A	19. A	29. B	39. D	49. D
10. C	20. D	30. D	40. A	50. C

TEST 2

DIRECTIONS: Each question or incomplete statement is followed by several suggested answers or completions. Select the one that BEST answers the question or completes the statement. *PRINT THE LETTER OF THE CORRECT ANSWER IN THE SPACE AT THE RIGHT.*

1. AMPLE

    A. necessary B. plentiful C. protected D. tasty

    1._____

2. EXPEDITE

    A. sue B. omit C. hasten D. verify

    2._____

3. FRAGMENT

    A. simple tool   B. broken part
    C. basic outline   D. weakness

    3._____

4. ADVERSARY

    A. thief B. partner C. loser D. foe

    4._____

5. ACHIEVE

    A. accomplish B. begin C. develop D. urge

    5._____

Questions 6-10.

DIRECTIONS: Answer Questions 6 to 10 on the basis of the information given in the table on the following page. The numbers which have been omitted from the table can be calculated from the other numbers which are given.

NUMBER OF DWELLING UNITS CONSTRUCTED

Year	Private one-family houses	In private apt. houses	In public housing	Total dwelling units
1996	4,500	500	600	5,600
1997	9,200	5,300	2,800	17,300
1998	8,900	12,800	6,800	28,500
1999	12,100	15,500	7,100	34,700
2000	?	12,200	14,100	39,200
2001	10,200	26,000	8,600	44,800
2002	10,300	17,900	7,400	35,600
2003	11,800	18,900	7,700	38,400
2004	12,700	22,100	8,400	43,200
2005	13,300	24,300	8,100	45,700
TOTALS	105,900	?	?	?

6. According to this table, the average number of public housing units constructed yearly during the period 1996 through 2005 was

    A. 7,160   B. 6,180   C. 7,610   D. 6,810

    6._____

7. Of the following, the two years in which the number of private one-family homes constructed was GREATEST for the two years together is

   A. 1998 and 1999
   B. 1997 and 2003
   C. 1998 and 2004
   D. 2001 and 2002

8. For the entire period of 1996 through 2005, the total of all private one-family houses constructed exceeded the total of all public housing units constructed by

   A. 34,300   B. 45,700   C. 50,000   D. 83,900

9. Of the total number of private apartment house dwelling units constructed in the ten years given in the table, the percentage which was constructed in 2002 was MOST NEARLY

   A. 5%   B. 11%   C. 16%   D. 21%

10. Considering dwelling units of all types, the average number constructed annually in the period from 2001 through 2005 was GREATER than the average number constructed annually in the period from 1996 through 2000 by

    A. 16,480   B. 33,320   C. 79,300   D. 82,400

11. A car speeds through the toll entrance of a 2 1/4 mile long bridge without paying the toll and reaches the other end of the bridge 1 minute and 30 seconds later. The car was traveling MOST NEARLY at a rate of _____ miles per hour.

    A. 60   B. 70   C. 80   D. 90

12. During one week, 21,500 vehicles passed through the toll booths of a certain bridge. Of these, 550 were buses, 2,230 were trucks, and the rest were passenger cars. The toll charges were $3.50 for a passenger car, $7 for a truck and $14 for a bus. The total income for the week was

    A. $80,850   B. $88,830   C. $102,550   D. $109,550

13. A bullet fired from a revolver travels 100 feet the first second, and each succeeding second it travels a distance 10% less than during the immediately preceding second. The number of feet the bullet will have traveled at the end of the fourth second is MOST NEARLY

    A. 272   B. 320   C. 344   D. 360

14. An officer receives a uniform allowance of $500 a year in a lump sum. Of this amount, he spends $180 for a winter jacket and 40% of the remainder for two pairs of trousers. The officer now wishes to buy a winter overcoat which costs $240.
    The percentage of the purchase price of the overcoat by which he will be short is

    A. 20%   B. 25%   C. 48%   D. 60%

15. It has been suggested that small light cars can be used for certain kinds of police work. These light vehicles can run 30 miles per gallon of gasoline as contrasted with standard cars which run only 15 miles per gallon. Assume gasoline costs the city $3.75 per gallon. During 9,000 miles of travel, use of the small light car in preference to the standard car would result in a saving in gasoline costs of MOST NEARLY

    A. $1,125   B. $1,500   C. $1,875   D. $2,250

16. Out of a total of 34,750 felony complaints in 2006, 14,200 involved burglary. In 2005, there was a total of 32,300 felony complaints of which 12,800 were burglary.
    Of the increase in felonies from 2005 to 2006, the increase in burglaries comprised APPROXIMATELY

    A. 27%   B. 37%   C. 47%   D. 57%

17. A certain city department has two offices which issue permits, one office handling twice as many applicants as the other. The smaller office grants permits to 40% of its applicants. The larger office handling twice as many applicants grants permits to 60% of its applicants.
    If there were 900 applicants at both offices together on a given day, the total number of permits granted by both offices would be MOST NEARLY

    A. 420   B. 450   C. 480   D. 510

18. If a co-worker is not breathing after receiving an electric shock but is no longer in contact with the electricity, it is MOST important for you to

    A. avoid moving him
    B. wrap the victim in a blanket
    C. start artificial respiration promptly
    D. force him to take hot liquids

19. Employees using supplies from one of the first-aid kits available throughout the building are required to submit an immediate report of the occurrence.
    Logical reasoning shows that the MOST important reason for this report is so that the

    A. supplies used will be sure to be replaced
    B. first-aid kit can be properly sealed again
    C. employee will be credited for his action
    D. record of first-aid supplies will be up-to-date

20. The BEST IMMEDIATE first-aid treatment for a scraped knee is to

    A. apply plain vaseline   B. wash it with soap and water
    C. apply heat   D. use a knee splint

21. Artificial respiration after a severe electrical shock is ALWAYS necessary when the shock results in

    A. unconsciousness   B. stoppage of breathing
    C. bleeding   D. a burn

22. The authority gives some of its maintenance employees instruction in first aid.
    The MOST likely reason for doing this is to

    A. eliminate the need for calling a doctor in case of accident
    B. provide temporary emergency treatment in case of accident
    C. lower the cost of accidents to the authority
    D. reduce the number of accidents

23. The BEST IMMEDIATE first aid if a chemical solution splashes into the eyes is to

    A. protect the eyes from the light by bandaging
    B. rub the eyes dry with a towel

C. cause tears to flow by staring at a bright light
D. flush the eyes with large quantities of clean water

24. If you had to telephone for an ambulance because of an accident, the MOST important information for you to give the person who answered the telephone would be the

    A. exact time of the accident
    B. cause of the accident
    C. place where the ambulance is needed
    D. names and addresses of those injured

25. If a person has a deep puncture wound in his finger caused by a sharp nail, the BEST IMMEDIATE first aid procedure would be to

    A. encourage bleeding by exerting pressure around the injured area
    B. stop all bleeding
    C. prevent air from reaching the wound
    D. probe the wound for steel particles

26. In addition to cases of submersion, artificial respiration is a recommended first aid procedure for

    A. sunstroke   B. electrical shock   C. chemical poisoning   D. apoplexy

27. Assume that you are called on to render first aid to a man injured in an accident. You find he is bleeding profusely, is unconscious, and has a broken arm. There is a strong odor of alcohol about him.
    The FIRST thing for which you should treat him is the

    A. bleeding   B. unconsciousness   C. broken arm   D. alcoholism

28. In applying first aid for removal of a foreign body in the eye, an important precaution to be observed is NOT to

    A. attempt to wash out the foreign body
    B. bring the upper eyelid down over the lower
    C. rub the eye
    D. touch or attempt to remove a speck on the lower lid

29. The one of the following symptoms which is LEAST likely to indicate that a person involved in an accident requires first aid for shock is that

    A. he has fainted twice
    B. his face is red and flushed
    C. his skin is wet with sweat
    D. his pulse is rapid

30. When giving first aid to a person suffering from shock as a result of an auto accident, it is MOST important to

    A. massage him in order to aid blood circulation
    B. have him sip whiskey
    C. prop him up in a sitting position
    D. cover the person and keep him warm

Questions 31-34.

DIRECTIONS: Answer questions 31 to 34 SOLELY on the basis of the following paragraph.

Assume that you are an officer assigned to one large office which issues and receives applications for various permits and licenses. The office consists of one section where the necessary forms are issued; another section where fees are paid to a cashier; and desks where applicants are interviewed and their forms reviewed and completed. There is also a section containing tables and chairs where persons may sit and fill out their applications before being interviewed or paying the fees. your duties consist of answering simple questions, directing the public to the correct section of the office, and maintaining order.

31. A man who speaks English poorly asks you for assistance in obtaining and filling out an application for a permit. You should

    A. send him to an interviewer who can assist him
    B. try to determine what permit he wants and fill out the form for him
    C. refer the man to the office supervisor
    D. ask another applicant to help this person

31._____

32. The office becomes noisy and crowded, with people milling around waiting for service at the various sections.
Of the following, the BEST action for you to take is to

    A. stand in a prominent place and in a loud voice request the people to be quiet
    B. direct all the people not being served to wait at the unoccupied tables until you call them
    C. line up the people in front of each section and keep the lines in good order
    D. tell the people to form a single line outside the office and let in a few at a time

32._____

33. A man who has just been denied a permit becomes angry and shouts that if he "knew the right people" he too could get a permit. His behavior is disturbing the office.
Of the following, the BEST action for you to take is to

    A. order the man to leave at once since his business is done
    B. tell the man to be quiet and file another application
    C. suggest to the supervisor that a pamphlet be prepared explaining the requirements for permits in simple language
    D. ask an interviewer to explain the requirements for his permit to the person and his right of appeal

33._____

34. Just before the close of business, a man rushes in and insists on being interviewed for a permit because his present one expires that night.
Of the following, the BEST action for you to take is to

    A. tell the man that the office is closed
    B. tell the man that there will be no penalty if he returns early the next morning
    C. inquire if an interviewer is still available to take care of him and send him to that desk
    D. tell the cashier to collect the fee and tell the man to return the next morning for an interview

34._____

35. Fingerprints are often taken of applicants for licenses. Of the following, the MOST valid reason for this procedure is that

    A. the license of someone who commits a crime can be more readily revoked
    B. applicants can be checked for possible criminal records
    C. it helps to make sure that the proper license fee is paid
    D. a complete employment record of the applicant is obtained

36. Assume that an officer is on patrol at 2 A.M. He notices that the night light inside one of the stores in a public building is out. The store is locked.
    Of the following, the FIRST action for him to take at this time is to

    A. continue on his patrol since the light probably burned out
    B. enter the store by any means possible so he can check it
    C. report the matter to his superior
    D. shine his flashlight through the window to look for anything unusual

37. In questioning a man suspected of having committed a theft, the BEST procedure for an officer to follow is to

    A. induce the man to express his feelings about the police, the courts, and his home environment
    B. threaten him with beatings when he refuses to answer your questions
    C. make any promises necessary to get him to confess
    D. remain calm and objective

38. As an officer, you are on duty in one of the offices of a large public building. A woman who has just finished her business with this office comes to you and reports that her son who was with her is missing.
    The one of the following which is the BEST action for you to take FIRST is to

    A. tell the mother that the child is probably all right and ask her to go to the local police station for help in finding the boy
    B. suggest that the mother wait in the office until the child turns up
    C. check nearby offices in an attempt to locate the child
    D. telephone the local police station and ask if any reports fitting the description of the child have been received

39. An officer assigned to patrol inside a public building at night has observed two men standing outside the doorway. Of the following, the MOST appropriate action for the officer to take FIRST is to

    A. approach the two men and ask them why they are standing there
    B. hide and wait for the two men to take some action
    C. phone the local police station and ask for help since these men may be planning criminal action
    D. check all the entrance doors of the building to make sure that they are locked

40. It is standard practice for special officers to inspect the restrooms in public buildings. This is done at regular intervals while on patrol.
    Of the following, the BEST reason for this practice is to

    A. inspect sanitary conditions
    B. discourage loiterers and potential criminals

C. check the ventilation
D. determine if all the equipment and plumbing is working properly

41. While on duty in the evening as an officer assigned to a public building, you receive a report that a card game is going on in one of the offices. Gambling is forbidden on government property.
Of the following, the BEST course of action for you to take is to

   A. go to the office and order the card players to leave
   B. ignore the complaint since this is probably just harmless social card playing
   C. report the matter to the building manager the next day
   D. go to the office and, if warranted, issue an appropriate warning

42. It has been suggested that special officers establish good working relationships with the local police officers of the police department on duty in the neighborhood.
Of the following, the MOST valid reason for this practice is that

   A. a spirit of good feeling and high morale will be created among members of the police department
   B. local police officers will probably cooperate more readily with the special officer
   C. local police officers can take over the building patrol duties of the special officer in case he is absent
   D. special officers have an even stronger obligation than ordinary citizens to cooperate with the police

43. It has been proposed that an officer assigned to a public building at night remain at one location in the building, instead of walking on patrol through the building.
This proposal is

   A. *bad;* chiefly because the officer would probably sit instead of stand at the proper location
   B. *good;* chiefly because the officer could do a better job of watching the entire building from one point
   C. *bad;* chiefly because anyone seeking to enter the building for illegal purposes might be able to do so at a point other than where the special officer is on duty
   D. *good;* chiefly because his supervisors would know exactly where to find him

44. In a busy office, an officer has been assigned the duty of making sure that the public is served in the order of their arrival at the office and that some employee is always taking care of a person desiring help.
Of the following, the BEST method for the officer to follow is to

   A. line up the persons in the waiting room
   B. give a numbered ticket to each person waiting and call out the numbers, in order, when an employee becomes available
   C. loudly announce "next" when an employee is available to serve someone
   D. seat one person next to each employee's desk and let the others wait for the first vacant seat

45. Two men have broken into and entered a building at night. The officer on duty at this building sees them, chases them out, and then observes them in the adjoining building.
    Of the following, the BEST course of action for the officer to take is to

    A. notify the local police station and be ready to aid the police
    B. enter the adjoining building to find the men
    C. notify the manager of his own building
    D. continue on duty since these men have left the building for which he is responsible

46. While an officer is on duty in a crowded waiting room, he finds a woman's purse on the floor.
    Of the following, the FIRST course of action for him to take is to

    A. hold it up in the air, ask who owns it, and give it to whoever claims it
    B. keep the purse until someone claims it
    C. immediately deliver the purse to the "lost and found" desk
    D. ask the lady who is nearest to him if she lost a purse

47. Special officers often have the power of arrest.
    Of the following, the BEST reason for this practice is to

    A. have the officer always arrest any person who refuses to obey his orders
    B. aid in maintaining order in places where he is assigned
    C. promote good public relations
    D. aid in preventing illegal use of public buildings by tenants or employees

48. An officer has told a mother that he found her son writing on the walls of the building with chalk. The mother tells the officer that he should be more concerned with "crooks" than with children's minor pranks.
    Of the following, the BEST answer for the officer to make to this woman is that

    A. children should be taught good conduct by their parents
    B. damage to public property means higher taxes
    C. serious criminals often begin their careers with minor violations
    D. it is his duty to enforce all rules and regulations

49. A man asks you, a special officer, where to get a certain kind of license not issued in your office. You don't know where such licenses are issued.
    Of the following, the BEST procedure for you to follow is to

    A. refer him to the manager of the office
    B. get the information if you can and give it to the man
    C. tell the man to inquire at any police station house
    D. tell the man that you just do not know

50. Special officers are not permitted to ask private citizens to buy tickets for dances or other such social functions, not even when such functions are operated by charitable organizations. Of the following, the BEST reason for this rule is that

    A. private citizens are under no obligation to buy any such tickets
    B. not all groups are allowed equal opportunity in the sale of their tickets
    C. private citizens might complain to officials
    D. private citizens might feel they would not get proper service unless they bought such tickets

KEY (CORRECT ANSWERS)

1. B	11. D	21. B	31. A	41. D
2. C	12. B	22. B	32. C	42. B
3. B	13. C	23. D	33. D	43. C
4. D	14. A	24. C	34. C	44. B
5. A	15. A	25. A	35. B	45. A
6. A	16. D	26. B	36. D	46. C
7. C	17. C	27. A	37. D	47. B
8. A	18. C	28. C	38. C	48. D
9. B	19. A	29. B	39. D	49. B
10. A	20. B	30. D	40. B	50. D

SOLUTIONS TO ARITHMETIC PROBLEMS

11. $2\frac{1}{4}$ miles are completed in 1 1/2 minutes (1 minute and 30 seconds)

    $\therefore 2\frac{1}{4} \div 1\frac{1}{2}$ = rate per minute

    $$= \frac{9}{4} \div 1\frac{1}{2}$$
    $$= \frac{9}{4} \div \frac{3}{2}$$
    $$= \frac{9}{4} \times \frac{2}{3}$$
    $$= \frac{3}{2} \text{ miles per minute}$$

    $\therefore \frac{3}{2} \times 60$ (minutes in an hour) = rate per hour = 90 miles per hour

    (Ans. D)

12. 550 + 2230 = 2780; 21,500 - 2780 = 18,720 passengers

550 buses at $14.00	=	$ 7,700
2230 trucks at $7.00	=	15,610
18720 passengers at $3.50	=	65,520
		$88,830

    (Ans. B)

13. Given: speed = 100 feet the first second

100 - 10 (10% of 100)	=	90 feet - the second second
90 - 9 (10% of 90)	=	81 feet - the third second
81 - 8.1 (10% of 81)	=	72.9 feet - the fourth second
		343.9 (total at end of the fourth second)

    (Ans. C)

14. Given: 500 = uniform allowance

$500 - 180	=	$320	(amount left after buying winter jacket)
$320 x 40%	=	$128	(amount spent for two pairs of trousers)
$320 - 128	=	$192	(amount now left)

    Since the winter overcoat costs $240, he is now short $48 ($240 - 192) or 20% of the purchase price of the overcoat. (48/240 = $\frac{1}{5}$ = 20%)

(Ans. A)

15. Light cars: 9000(miles)÷30(miles per gallon)×3.75(per gallon)

$$= \frac{9000}{30} \times 3.75$$
$$= 300 \times 3.75$$
$$= \$1,125 \text{ (total gasoline cost)}$$

Standard cars: 9000 (miles) ÷ 15 (miles per gallon) × 3.75

$$= \frac{9000}{15} \times 3.75$$
$$= 600 \times 3.75$$
$$= \$2,250 \text{ (total gasoline cost)}$$

∴ use of light car would result in a saving in gasoline costs of $1,125 ($2,250 - $1,125).

(Ans. A)

16.
2006:	14,200	(burglary)
2005:	12,800	(burglary)
	1,400	(increase in burglaries)

2006:	34,750	(felony)
2005:	32,300	(felony)
	2,450	(increase in felonies

$$\therefore 1400 \div 2450 = \frac{1400}{2450} = .57$$

WORK

```
         .57
     ┌────────
2450 )1400.0
      1225.0
      ──────
       175.00
       171.50
```

(Ans. D)

17. Given: smaller office: grants permits to 40% of 1/3 of the total number of applicants (900)

larger office: grants permits to 60% of 2/3 of the total number of applicants (900)

Solving: smaller office: $.40 \times \frac{1}{3} \times 900 = 120$ permits

larger office: $.60 \times \frac{2}{3} \times 900 = 360$ permits
                                              480 permits (total)

(Ans. C)

EXAMINATION SECTION
TEST 1

DIRECTIONS: Each question or incomplete statement is followed by several suggested answers or completions. Select the one that BEST answers the question or completes the statement. *PRINT THE LETTER OF THE CORRECT ANSWER IN THE SPACE AT THE RIGHT.*

Questions 1-4.

DIRECTIONS: Questions 1 through 4 are based on the picture entitled *Contents of a Woman's Handbag.* Assume that all of the contents are shown in the picture.

<u>CONTENTS OF A WOMAN'S HANDBAG</u>

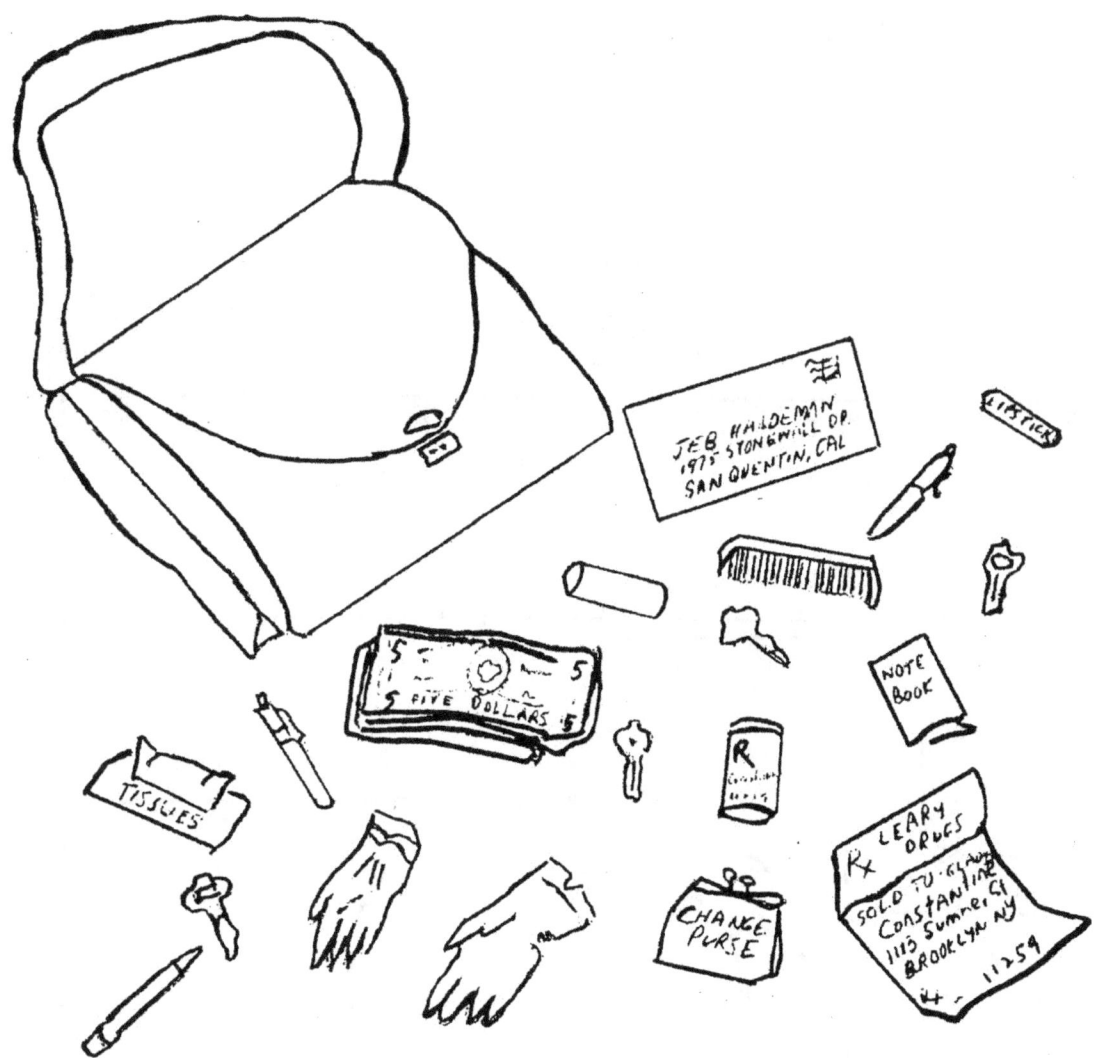

1. Where does Gladys Constantine live?

   A. Chalmers Street in Manhattan
   B. Summer Street in Manhattan
   C. Summer Street in Brooklyn
   D. Chalmers Street in Brooklyn

2. How many keys were in the handbag?

   A. 2 B. 3 C. 4 D. 5

3. How much money was in the handbag? _____ dollar(s).

   A. Exactly five
   B. More than five
   C. Exactly ten
   D. Less than one

4. The sales slip found in the handbag shows the purchase of which of the following?

   A. The handbag
   B. Lipstick
   C. Tissues
   D. Prescription medicine

Questions 5-8.

DIRECTIONS: Questions 5 through 8 are based on the floor plan below.

FLOOR PLAN

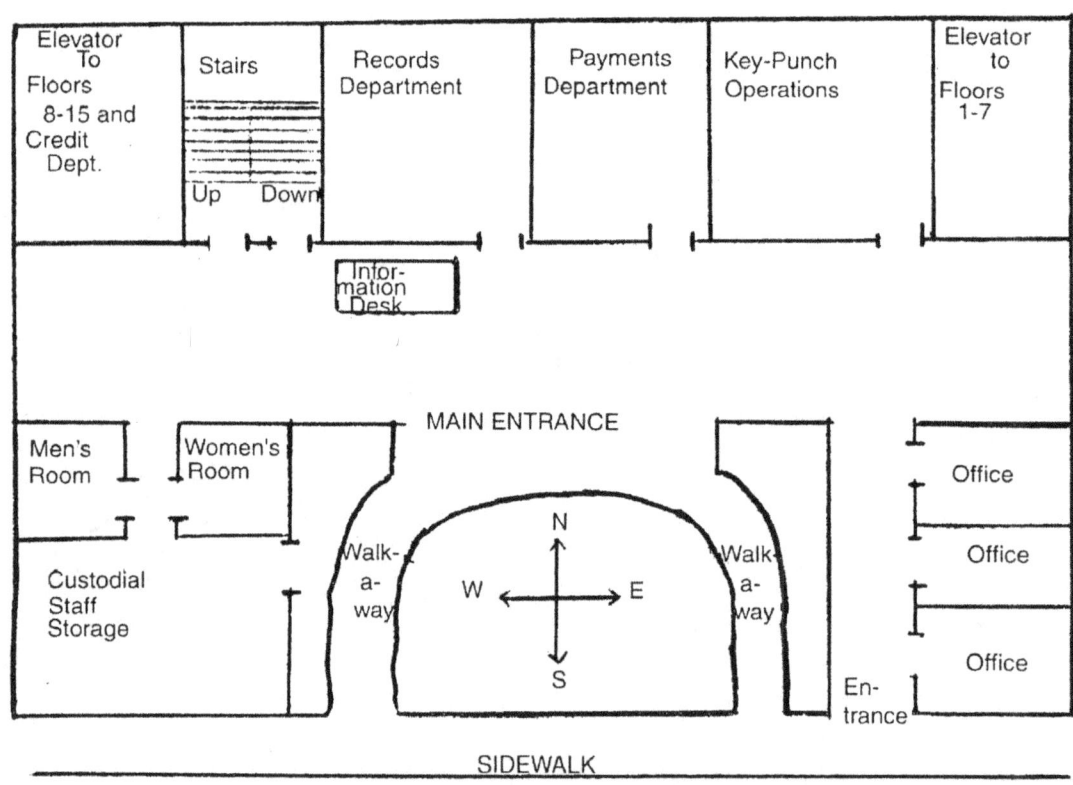

5. A special officer (security officer) on duty at the main entrance must be aware of other outside entrances to his area of the building. These unguarded entrances are usually kept locked, but they are important in case of fire or other emergency.
Besides the main entrance, how many OTHER entrances shown on the floor plan directly face Forty-ninth Street?
_____ other entrances.

   A. No   B. One   C. Two   D. Three

6. A person who arrives at the main entrance and asks to be directed to the Credit Department SHOULD be told to

   A. take the elevator on the left
   B. take the elevator on the right
   C. go to a different entrance
   D. go up the stairs on the left

7. On the east side of the entrance can be found

   A. a storage room   B. offices
   C. toilets   D. stairs

8. The space DIRECTLY BEHIND the Information Desk in the floor plan is occupied by

   A. up and down stairs   B. key punch operations
   C. toilets   D. the records department

Questions 9-12.

DIRECTIONS: Answer Questions 9 to 12 on the basis of the information given in the passage below.

The public often believes that the main job of a uniformed officer is to enforce laws by simply arresting people. In reality, however, many of the situations that an officer deals with do not call for the use of his arrest power. In the first place, an officer spends much of his time <u>preventing</u> crimes from happening, by spotting potential violations or suspicious behavior and taking action to prevent illegal acts. In the second place, many of the situations in which officers are called on for assistance involve elements like personal arguments, husband-wife quarrels, noisy juveniles, or mentally disturbed persons. The majority of these problems do not result in arrests and convictions, and often they do not even involve illegal behavior. In the third place, even in situations where there seems to be good reason to make an arrest, an officer may have to exercise very good judgment. There are times when making an arrest too soon could touch off a riot, or could result in the detention of a minor offender while major offenders escaped, or could cut short the gathering of necessary on-the-scene evidence.

9. The above passage IMPLIES that most citizens

   A. will start to riot if they see an arrest being made
   B. appreciate the work that law enforcement officers do
   C. do not realize that making arrests is only a small part of law enforcement
   D. never call for assistance unless they are involved in a personal argument or a husband-wife quarrel

10. According to the passage, one way in which law enforcement officers can prevent crimes from happening is by

   A. arresting suspicious characters
   B. letting minor offenders go free
   C. taking action on potential violations
   D. refusing to get involved in husband-wife fights

11. According to the passage, which of the following statements is NOT true of situations involving mentally disturbed persons?

   A. It is a waste of time to call on law enforcement officers for assistance in such situations.
   B. Such situations may not involve illegal behavior
   C. Such situations often do not result in arrests.
   D. Citizens often turn to law enforcement officers for help in such situations.

12. The last sentence in the passage mentions *detention of minor offenders.*
    Of the following, which BEST explains the meaning of the word *detention* as used here?

   A. Sentencing someone
   B. Indicting someone
   C. Calling someone before a grand jury
   D. Arresting someone

Questions 13-28.

DIRECTIONS: In answering Questions 13 through 28, assume that *you* means a special officer (security officer) on duty. Your basic responsibilities are safeguarding people and property and maintaining order in the area to which you are assigned. You are in uniform, and you are not armed. You keep in touch with your supervisory station either by telephone or by a two-way radio (walkie-talkie).

13. It is a general rule that if the security alarm goes off showing that someone has made an unlawful entrance into a building, no officer responsible for security shall proceed to investigate alone. Each officer must be accompanied by at least one other officer.
    Of the following, which is the MOST probable reason for this rule?

   A. It is dangerous for an officer to investigate such a situation alone.
   B. The intruder might try to bribe an officer to let him go.
   C. One officer may be inexperienced and needs an experienced partner.
   D. Two officers are better than one officer in writing a report of the investigation.

14. You are on weekend duty on the main floor of a public building. The building is closed to the public on weekends, but some employees are sometimes asked to work weekends. You have been instructed to use cautious good judgment in opening the door for such persons.
    Of the following, which one MOST clearly shows the poorest judgment?

A. Admitting an employee who is personally known to you without asking to see any identification except the permit slip signed by the employee's supervisor
B. Refusing to admit someone whom you do not recognize but who claims left his identification at home
C. Admitting to the building only those who can give a detailed description of their weekend work duties
D. Leaving the entrance door locked for a while to make regulation security checks of other areas in the building with the result that no one can either enter or leave during these periods

15. You are on duty at a public building. An office employee tells you that she left her purse in her desk when she went out to lunch, and she has just discovered that it is gone. She has been back from lunch for half an hour and has not left her desk during this period. What should you do FIRST?

    A. Warn all security personnel to stop any suspicious-looking person who is seen with a purse
    B. Ask for a description of the purse
    C. Call the Lost and Found and ask if a purse has been turned in
    D. Obtain statements from any employees who were in the office during the lunch hour

16. You are patrolling your assigned area in a public building. You hear a sudden crash and the sound of running footsteps. You investigate and find that someone has forced open a locked entrance to the building. What is the FIRST thing you should do?

    A. Close the door and try to fix the lock so that no one else can get in
    B. Use your two-way radio to report the emergency and summon help
    C. Chase after the person whose running footsteps you heard
    D. Go immediately to your base office and make out a brief written report

17. You and another special officer (security officer) are on duty in the main waiting area at a welfare center. A caseworker calls both of you over and whispers that one of the clients, Richard Roe, may be carrying a gun. Of the following, what is the BEST action for both of you to take?

    A. You should approach the man, one on each side, and one of you should say loudly and clearly, *"Richard Roe, you are under arrest."*
    B. Both of you should ask the man to go with you to a private room, and then find out if he is carrying a gun
    C. Both of you should grab him, handcuff him, and take him to the nearest precinct station house
    D. Both of you should watch him carefully but not do anything unless he actually pulls a gun

18. You are on duty at a welfare center. You are told that a caseworker is being threatened by a man with a knife. You go immediately to the scene, and you find the caseworker lying on the floor with blood spurting from a wound in his arm. You do not know who the attacker is. What should you do FIRST?

    A. Ask the caseworker for a description of the attacker so that you can set out in pursuit and try to catch him
    B. Take down the names and addresses of any witnesses to the incident

C. Give first aid to the caseworker, if you can, and immediately call for an ambulance
D. Search the people standing around in the room for the knife

19. As a special officer (security officer), you have been patrolling a special section of a hospital building for a week. Smoking is not allowed in this section because the oxygen tanks in use here could easily explode. However, you have observed that some employees sneak into the linen-supply room in this section in order to smoke without anybody seeing them.
Of the following, which is the BEST way for you to deal with this situation?

    A. Whenever you catch anyone smoking, call his supervisor immediately
    B. Request the Building Superintendent to put a padlock on the door of the linen-supply room
    C. Ignore the smoking because you do not want to get a reputation for interfering in the private affairs of other employees
    D. Report the situation to your supervisor and follow his instructions

20. You are on duty at a hospital. You have been assigned to guard the main door, and you are responsible for remaining at your post until relieved. On one of the wards for which you are not responsible, there is a patient who was wounded in a street fight. This patient is under arrest for killing another man in this fight, and he is supposed to be under round-the-clock police guard. A nurse tells you that one of the police officers assigned to guard the patient has suddenly taken ill and has to periodically leave his post to go to the washroom. The nurse is worried because she thinks the patient might try to escape.
Of the following, which is the BEST action for you to take?

    A. Tell the nurse to call you whenever the police officer leaves his post so that you can keep an eye on the patient while the officer is gone
    B. Assume that the police officer probably knows his job, and that there is no reason for you to worry
    C. Alert your supervisor to the nurse's report
    D. Warn the police officer that the nurse has been talking about him

21. You are on night duty at a hospital where you are responsible for patrolling a large section of the main building. Your supervisor tells you that there have been several nighttime thefts from a supply room in your section and asks you to be especially alert for suspicious activity near this supply room.
Of the following, which is the MOST reasonable way to carry out your supervisor's direction?

    A. Check the supply room regularly at half-hour intervals
    B. Make frequent checks of the supply room at irregular intervals
    C. Station yourself by the door of the supply room and stay at this post all night
    D. Find a hidden spot from which you can watch the supply room and stay there all night

22. You are on duty at a vehicle entrance to a hospital. Parking space on the hospital grounds is strictly limited, and no one is ever allowed to park there unless they have an official parking permit. You have just stopped a driver who does not have a parking permit, but he explains that
he is a doctor and he has a patient in the hospital. What should you do?

A. Let him park since he has explained that he is a doctor
B. Ask in a friendly way, *"Can I check your identification?"*
C. Call the Information Desk to make sure there is such a patient in the hospital
D. Tell the driver politely but firmly that he will have to park somewhere else

23. You are on duty at a public building. A man was just mugged on a stairway. The mugger took the man's wallet and started to run down the stairs but tripped and fell. Now the mugger is lying unconscious at the bottom of the stairs and bleeding from the mouth.
The FIRST thing you should do is to

 A. search him to see if he is carrying any other stolen property
 B. pick him up and carry him away from the stairs
 C. try and revive him for questioning
 D. put in a call for an ambulance and police assistance

24. After someone breaks into an employee's locker at a public building, you interview the employee to determine what is missing from the locker. The employee becomes hysterical and asks why you are *wasting time with all these questions* instead of going after the thief.
The MOST reasonable thing for you to do is

 A. tell the employee that it is very important to have an accurate description of the missing articles
 B. quietly tell the employee to calm down and stop interfering with your work
 C. explain to the employee that you are only doing what you were told to do and that you don't make the rules
 D. assure the employee that there are a lot of people working on the case and that someone else is probably arresting the thief right now

25. You are on duty at a public building. An employee reports that a man has just held her up and taken her money. The employee says that the man was about 25 years old, with short blond hair and a pale complexion and was wearing blue jeans.
Of the following additional facts, which one would probably be MOST valuable to officers searching the building for the suspect?

 A. The man was wearing dark glasses.
 B. He had on a green jacket.
 C. He was about 5 feet 8 inches tall.
 D. His hands and fingernails were very dirty.

26. When the fire alarm goes off, it is your job as a special officer (security officer) to see that all employees leave the building quickly by the correct exits. A fire alarm has just sounded, and you are checking the offices on one of the floors. A supervisor in one office tells you, *"This is probably just another fire drill. I've sent my office staff out, but I don't want to stop my own work."*
What should you do?

 A. Insist politely but firmly that the supervisor must obey the fire rules.
 B. Tell the supervisor that it is all right this time but that the rules must be followed in the future.
 C. Tell the supervisor that he is under arrest.
 D. Allow the supervisor to do as he sees fit since he is in charge of his own office.

27. You are on duty on the main floor of a public building. You have been informed that a briefcase has just been stolen from an office on the tenth floor. You see a man getting off the elevator with a briefcase that matches the description of the one that was stolen. What is the FIRST action you should take?

    A. Arrest the man and take him to the nearest public station
    B. Stop the man and say politely that you want to take a look at the briefcase
    C. Take the briefcase from the man and tell him that he cannot have it back unless he can prove that it is his
    D. Do not stop the man but note down his description and the exact time he got off the elevator

28. You are on duty at a welfare center. You have been told that two clients are arguing with a caseworker and making loud threats. You go to the scene, but the caseworker tells you that everything is now under control. The two clients, who are both mean-looking characters, are still there but seem to be acting normally.
What SHOULD you do?

    A. Apologize for having made a mistake and go away.
    B. Arrest the two men for having caused a disturbance.
    C. Insist on standing by until the interview is over, then escort the two men from the building.
    D. Leave the immediate scene but watch for any further developments.

29. You are on duty at a welfare center. A client comes up to you and says that two men just threatened him with a knife and made him give them his money. The client has alcohol on his breath and he is shabbily dressed. He points out the two men he says took the money.
Of the following, which is the BEST action to take?

    A. Arrest the two men on the client's complaint.
    B. Ignore the client's complaint since he doesn't look as if he could have had any money.
    C. Suggest to the client that he may be imagining things.
    D. Investigate and find out what happened.

Questions 30-35.

DIRECTIONS: Answer Questions 30 through 35 on the basis of the information given in the passage below. Assume that all questions refer to the same state described in the passage.

The courts and the police consider an "offense" as any conduct that is punishable by a fine or imprisonment. Such offenses include many kinds of acts - from behavior that is merely annoying, like throwing a noisy party that keeps everyone awake, all the way up to violent acts like murder. The law classifies offenses according to the penalties that are provided for them. In one state, minor offenses are called "violations." A violation is punishable by a fine of not more than $250 or imprisonment of not more than. 15 days, or both. The annoying behavior mentioned above is an example of a violation. More serious offenses are classified as "crimes." Crimes are classified by the kind of penalty that is provided. A "misdemeanor" is a crime that is punishable by a fine of not more than $1,000 or by imprisonment of not more than one year, or both. Examples of misdemeanors include stealing something with a value of $100 or less, turning in a false alarm, or illegally possessing less than 1/8 of an ounce of a dangerous drug. A "felony" is a criminal offense punishable by imprisonment of more than one year. Murder is clearly a felony.

30. According to the above passage, any act that is punishable by imprisonment or by a fine is called a(n)

    A. offense B. violation C. crime D. felony

31. According to the above passage, which of the following is classified as a crime?

    A. Offense punishable by 15 days imprisonment
    B. Minor offense
    C. Violation
    D. Misdemeanor

32. According to the above passage, if a person guilty of burglary can receive a prison sentence of 7 years or more, burglary would be classified as a

    A. violation B. misdemeanor
    C. felony D. violent act

33. According to the above passage, two offenses that would BOTH be classified as misdemeanors are

    A. making unreasonable noise and stealing a $90 bicycle
    B. stealing a $75 radio and possessing 1/16 of an ounce of heroin
    C. holding up a bank and possessing 1/4 of a pound of marijuana
    D. falsely reporting a fire and illegally double-parking

34. The above passage says that offenses are classified according to the penalties provided for them.
    On the basis of clues in the passage, who probably decides what the maximum penalties should be for the different kinds of offenses?

    A. The State lawmakers B. The City police
    C. The Mayor D. Officials in Washington, B.C.

35. Of the following, which BEST describes the subject matter of the passage?

    A. How society deals with criminals
    B. How offenses are classified
    C. Three types of criminal behavior
    D. The police approach to offenders

KEY (CORRECT ANSWERS)

1.	C	16.	B
2.	C	17.	B
3.	B	18.	C
4.	D	19.	D
5.	B	20.	C
6.	A	21.	B
7.	B	22.	D
8.	D	23.	D
9.	C	24.	A
10.	C	25.	C
11.	A	26.	A
12.	D	27.	B
13.	A	28.	D
14.	C	29.	D
15.	B	30.	A

31. D
32. C
33. B
34. A
35. B

TEST 2

DIRECTIONS: Each question or incomplete statement is followed by several suggested answers or completions. Select the one that BEST answers the question or completes the statement. *PRINT THE LETTER OF THE CORRECT ANSWER IN THE SPACE AT THE RIGHT.*

Questions 1-5.

DIRECTIONS: Questions 1 through 5 are based on the drawing below showing a view of a waiting area in a public building.

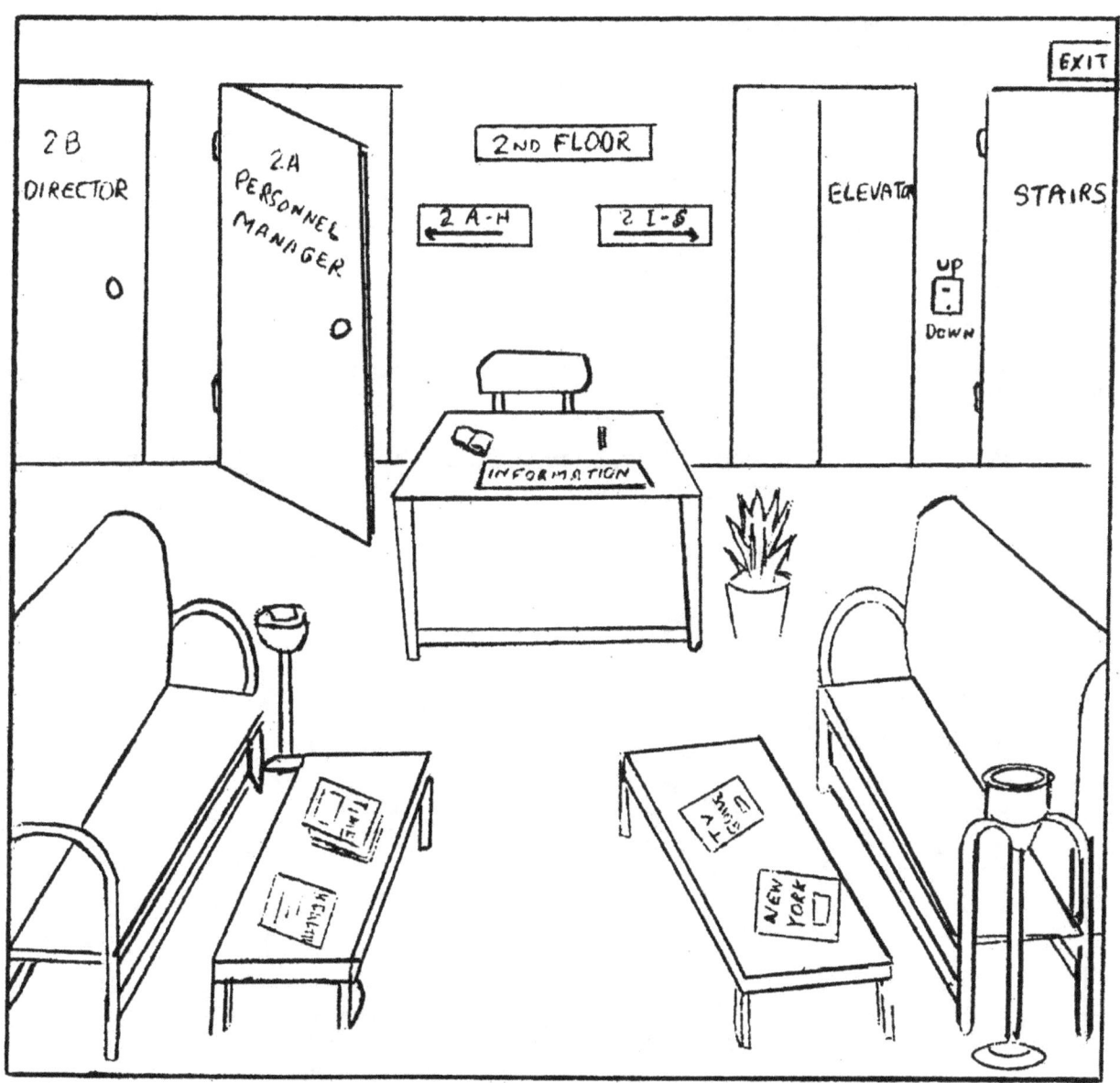

1. A desk is shown in the drawing. Which of the following is on the desk? A(n) 1.____

    A. plant   B. telephone
    C. In-Out file   D. *Information* sign

33

2. On which floor is the waiting area?

   A. Basement
   B. Main floor
   C. Second floor
   D. Third floor

3. The door IMMEDIATELY TO THE RIGHT of the desk is a(n)

   A. door to the Personnel Office
   B. elevator door
   C. door to another corridor
   D. door to the stairs

4. Among the magazines on the tables in the waiting area are

   A. TIME and NEWSWEEK
   B. READER'S DIGEST and T.V. GUIDE
   C. NEW YORK and READER'S DIGEST
   D. TIME and T.V. GUIDE

5. One door is partly open. This is the door to

   A. the Director's office
   B. the Personnel Manager's office
   C. the stairs
   D. an unmarked office

Questions 6-9.

DIRECTIONS: Questions 6 through 9 are based on the drawing below showing the contents of a male suspect's pockets.

CONTENTS OF A MALE SUSPECT'S POCKETS

6. The suspect had a slip in his pockets showing an appointment at an out-patient clinic on 6.____

   A. February 9, 2013 B. September 2, 2013
   C. February 19, 2013 D. September 12, 2013

7. The MP3 player that was found on the suspect was made by 7.____

   A. RCA B. GE C. Sony D. Zenith

8. The coins found in the suspect's pockets have a TOTAL value of 8.____

   A. 56¢ B. 77¢ C. $1.05 D. $1.26

9. All except one of the following were found in the suspect's pockets. 9.____
   Which was NOT found? A

   A. ticket stub B. comb
   C. subway fare D. pen

Questions 10-18

DIRECTIONS: In answering Questions 10 through 18, assume that *you* means a special officer (security officer) on duty. Your basic responsibilities are safeguarding people and property and maintaining order in the area to which you are assigned. You are in uniform, and you are not armed. You keep in touch with your supervisory station either by telephone or by a two-way radio (a walkie-talkie).

10. You are on duty at a center run by the Department of Social Services. Two teenaged 10.____
    boys are on their way out of the center. As they go past you, they look at you and laugh, and one makes a remark to you in Spanish. You do not understand Spanish, but you suspect it was a nasty remark.
    What SHOULD you do?

    A. Give the boys a lecture about showing respect for a uniform.
    B. Tell the boys that they had better stay away from the center from now on.
    C. Call for an interpreter and insist that the boy repeat the remark to the interpreter.
    D. Let the boys go on their way since they have done nothing requiring your intervention.

11. You are on duty at a shelter run by the Department of Social Services. You know that 11.____
    many of the shelter clients have drinking problems, drug problems, or mental health problems. You get a call for assistance from a caseworker who says a fight has broken out. When you arrive on the scene, you see that about a dozen clients are engaged in a free-for-all and that two or three of them have pulled knives.
    The BEST course of action is to

    A. call for additional assistance and order all bystanders away from the area
    B. jump into the center of the fighting group and try to separate the fighters
    C. pick up a heavy object and start swinging at anybody who has a knife
    D. try to find out what clients started the fight and place them under arrest

12. You have been assigned to duty at a children's shelter run by the Department of Social Services. The children range in age from 6 to 15, and many of them are at the shelter because they have no homes to go to.
    Of the following, which is the BEST attitude for you to take in dealing with these youngsters?

    A. Assume that they admire and respect anyone in uniform and that they will not usually give you much trouble
    B. Assume that they fear and distrust anyone in uniform and that they are going to give you a hard time unless you act tough
    C. Expect that many of them are going to become juvenile delinquents because of their bad backgrounds and that you should be suspicious of everything they do
    D. Expect that many of them may be emotionally upset and that you should be alert for unusual behavior

13. You are on duty outside the emergency room of a hospital. You notice that an old man has been sitting on a bench outside the room for a long time. He arrived alone, and he has not spoken to anyone at all.
    What SHOULD you do?

    A. Pay no attention to him since he is not bothering anyone.
    B. Tell him to leave since he does not seem to have any business there.
    C. Ask him if you can help him in any way.
    D. Do not speak to him, but keep an eye on him.

14. You are patrolling a section of a public building. An elderly woman carrying a heavy shopping bag asks you if you would watch the shopping bag for her while she keeps an appointment in the building.
    What SHOULD you do?

    A. Watch the shopping bag for her since her appointment probably will not take long.
    B. Refuse her request, explaining that your duties keep you on the move.
    C. Agree to her request just to be polite, but then continue your patrol after the woman is out of sight.
    D. Find a bystander who will agree to watch the shopping bag for her.

15. You are on duty at a public building. It is nearly 6:00 P.M., and most employees have left for the day.
    You see two well-dressed men carrying an office calculating machine out of the building. You SHOULD

    A. stop them and ask for an explanation
    B. follow them to see where they are going
    C. order them to put down the machine and leave the building immediately
    D. take no action since they do not look like burglars

16. You are on duty patrolling a public building. You have just tripped on the stairs and turned your ankle. The ankle hurts and is starting to swell.
    What is the BEST thing to do?

A. Take a taxi to a hospital emergency room, and from there have a hospital employee call your supervisor to explain the situation.
B. First try soaking your foot in cold water for half an hour, then go off duty if you really cannot walk at all.
C. Report the situation to your supervisor, explaining that you need prompt medical attention for your ankle.
D. Find a place where you can sit until you are due to go off duty, then have a doctor look at your ankle.

17. One of your duties as a special officer (security officer) on night patrol in a public building is to check the washrooms to see that the taps are turned off and that there are no plumbing leaks.
Of the following possible reasons for this inspection, which is probably the MOST important reason?

    A. If the floor gets wet, someone might slip and fall the next morning.
    B. A running water tap might be a sign that there is an intruder in the building.
    C. A washroom flood could leak through the ceilings and walls below and cause a lot of damage.
    D. Leaks must be reported quickly so that repairs can be scheduled as soon as possible.

18. You are on duty at a public building. A department supervisor tells you that someone has left a suspicious-looking package in the hallway on his floor. You investigate, and you hear ticking in the parcel. You think it could be a bomb.
The FIRST thing you should do is to

    A. rapidly question employees on this floor to get a description of the person who left the package
    B. write down the description of the package and the name of the department supervisor
    C. notify your security headquarters that there may be a bomb in the building and that all personnel should be evacuated
    D. pick up the package carefully and remove it from the building as quickly as you can

Questions 19-22.

DIRECTIONS: Answer Questions 19 through 22 on the basis of the Fact Situation and the Report of Arrest form below. Questions 19 through 22 ask how the report form should be filled in based on the information given in the Fact Situation.

FACT SITUATION

Jesse Stein is a special officer (security officer) who is assigned to a welfare center at 435 East Smythe Street, Brooklyn. He was on duty there Thursday morning, February 1. At 10:30 A.M., a client named Jo Ann Jones, 40 years old, arrived with her ten-year-old son, Peter. Another client, Mary Alice Wiell, 45 years old, immediately began to insult Mrs. Jones. When Mrs. Jones told her to "go away," Mrs. Wiell pulled out a long knife. The special officer (security officer) intervened and requested Mrs. Wiell to drop the knife. She would not, and he had to use necessary force to disarm her. He arrested her on charges of disorderly conduct, harassment, and possession of a dangerous weapon. Mrs. Wiell lives at 118 Heally Street,

Brooklyn, Apartment 4F, and she is unemployed. The reason for her aggressive behavior is not known.

```
REPORT OF ARREST
01) _____   (08) _____
    (Prisoner's surname) (first) (initial)    (Precinct)
02) _____   (09) _____
    (Address)                                 (Date of arrest)
                                              (Month, Day)
03) _____ (04) _____ (05) _____  (10) _____
    (Date of birth) (Age)   (Sex)             (Time of arrest)
06) _____ (07) _____   (11) _____
    (Occupation)    (Where employed)          (Place of arrest)

(12) _____
     (Specific offenses)

(13) _____    (14) _____
     (Arresting Officer)                     (Officer's No.)
```

19. What entry should be made in Blank 01?

    A. Jo Ann Jones B. Jones, Jo Ann
    C. Mary Wiell   D. Wiell, Mary A.

20. Which of the following should be entered in Blank 04?

    A. 40   B. 40's   C. 45   D. Middle-aged

21. Which of the following should be entered in Blank 09?

    A. Wednesday, February 1, 10:30 A.M.
    B. February 1
    C. Thursday morning, February 2
    D. Morning, February 4

22. Of the following, which would be the BEST entry to make in Blank 11?

    A. Really Street Welfare Center
    B. Brooklyn
    C. 435 E. Smythe St., Brooklyn
    D. 118 Heally St., Apt. 4F

Questions 23-27.

DIRECTIONS: Answer Questions 23 through 27 on the basis of the information given in the Report of Loss or Theft that appears below.

```
REPORT OF LOSS OR THEFT          Date: 12/4      Time: 9:15 a.m.
Complaint made by:  Richard Aldridge          ☐ Owner
                    306 S. Walter St.         ☒ Other - explain:
                                              Head of Accty. Dept.

Type of property: Computer                    Value: $550.00
Description: Dell
Location: 768 N Margin Ave., Accounting Dept., 3rd Floor
Time: Overnight 12/3 - 12/4
Circumstances: Mr. Aldridge reports he arrived at work 8:45 A.M.,
found office door open and machine missing. Nothing else reported
missing. I investigated and found signs of forced entry: door lock
was broken.           Signature of Reporting Officer: B.L. Ramirez
Notify:
  ☐ Building & Grounds Office, 768 N. Margin Ave.
  ☐ Lost Property Office, 110 Brand Ave.
  ☒ Security Office, 703 N. Wide Street
```

23. The person who made this complaint is

    A. a secretary
    B. a security officer
    C. Richard Aldridge
    D. B.L. Ramirez

24. The report concerns a computer that has been

    A. lost   B. damaged   C. stolen   D. sold

25. The person who took the computer probably entered the office through

    A. a door   B. a window   C. the roof   D. the basement

26. When did the head of the Accounting Department first notice that the computer was missing?

    A. December 4 at 9:15 A.M.
    B. December 4 at 8:45 A.M.
    C. The night of December 3
    D. The night of December 4

27. The event described in the report took place at

    A. 306 South Walter Street
    B. 768 North Margin Avenue
    C. 110 Brand Avenue
    D. 703 North Wide Street

Questions 28-33.

DIRECTIONS: Answer Questions 28 through 33 on the basis of the instructions, the code, and the sample question given below.

Assume that a special officer (security officer) at a certain location is equipped with a two-way radio to keep him in constant touch with his security headquarters. Radio messages and replies are given in code form, as follows:

Radio Code for Situation	J	P	M	F	B
Radio Code for Action to be Taken	o	r	a	z	q
Radio Response for Action Being Taken	1	2	3	4	5

Assume that each of the above capital letters is the radio code for a particular type of situation, that the small letter below each capital letter is the radio code for the action a special officer (security officer) is directed to take, and that the number directly below each small letter is the radio response a special officer (security officer) should make to indicate what action was actually taken.

In each of the following Questions 28 through 33, the code letter for the action directed (Column 2) and the code number for the action taken (Column 3) should correspond to the capital letters in Column 1.

If only Column 2 is different from Column 1, mark your answer A.

If only Column 3 is different from Column 1, mark your answer B.

If both Column 2 and Column 3 are different from Column 1, mark your answer C.

If both Columns 2 and 3 are the same as Column 1, mark your answer D.

SAMPLE QUESTION

Column 1	Column 2	Column 3
JPFMB	orzaq	12453

The code letters in Column 2 are correct, but the numbers 53 in Column 3 should be 35. Therefore, the answer is B.

	Column 1	Column 2	Column 3	
28.	PBFJM	rqzoa	25413	28.____
29.	MPFBJ	zrqao	32541	29.____
30.	JBFPM	oqzra	15432	30.____
31.	BJPMF	qaroz	51234	31.____
32.	PJFMB	rozaq	21435	32.____
33.	FJBMP	zoqra	41532	33.____

Questions 34-40.

DIRECTIONS: Questions 34 through 40 are based on the instructions given below. Study the instructions and the sample question; then answer Questions 34 through 40 on the basis of this information

INSTRUCTIONS:

In each of the following Questions 34 through 40, the 3-line name and address in Column 1 is the master-list entry, and the 3-line entry in Column 2 is the information to be checked against the master list.

If there is one line that does not match, mark your answer A.

If there are two lines that do not match, mark your answer B.

If all three lines do not match, mark your answer C.

If the lines all match exactly, mark your answer D.

SAMPLE QUESTION:

Column 1
Mark L. Field
11-09 Prince Park Blvd.
Bronx, N.Y. 11402

Column 2
Mark L. Field
11-99 Prince Park
Bronx, N.Y. 11401

The first lines in each column match exactly. The second lines do not match, since 11-09 does not match 11-99 and Blvd. does not match Way. The third lines do not match either, since 11402 does not match 11401. Therefore, there are two lines that do not match and the correct answer is B.

	Column 1	Column 2	
34.	Jerome A. Jackson 1243 14th Avenue New York, N.Y. 10023	Jerome A. Johnson 1234 14th Avenue New York, N.Y. 10023	34.____
35.	Sophie Strachtheim 33-28 Connecticut Ave. Far Rockaway, N.Y. 11697	Sophie Strachtheim 33-28 Connecticut Ave. Far Rockaway, N.Y. 11697	35.____
36.	Elisabeth N.T. Gorrell 256 Exchange St. New York, N.Y. 10013	Elizabeth N.T. Gorrell 256 Exchange St. New York, N.Y. 10013	36.____
37.	Maria J. Gonzalez 7516 E. Sheepshead Rd. Brooklyn, N.Y. 11240	Maria J. Gonzalez 7516 N. Shepshead Rd. Brooklyn, N.Y. 11240	37.____
38.	Leslie B. Brautenweiler 21 57A Seller Terr. Flushing, N.Y. 11367	Leslie B. Brautenwieler 21-75A Seiler Terr. Flushing, N.J. 11367	38.____

39. Rigoberto J. Peredes Rigoberto J. Peredes 39.____
    157 Twin Towers, #18F 157 Twin Towers, #18F
    Tottenville, S.I., N.Y. Tottenville, S.I., N.Y.

40. Pietro F. Albino Pietro F. Albina 40.____
    P.O. Box 7548 P.O. Box 7458
    Floral Park, N.Y. 11005 Floral Park, N.Y. 11005

KEY (CORRECT ANSWERS)

1.	D	11.	A	21.	B	31.	A
2.	C	12.	D	22.	C	32.	D
3.	B	13.	C	23.	C	33.	A
4.	D	14.	B	24.	C	34.	B
5.	B	15.	A	25.	A	35.	D
6.	A	16.	C	26.	B	36.	A
7.	C	17.	C	27.	B	37.	A
8.	D	18.	C	28.	D	38.	C
9.	D	19.	D	29.	C	39.	D
10.	D	20.	C	30.	B	40.	B

EXAMINATION SECTION
TEST 1

DIRECTIONS: Each question or incomplete statement is followed by several suggested answers or completions. Select the one that BEST answers the question or completes the statement. *PRINT THE LETTER OF THE CORRECT ANSWER IN THE SPACE AT THE RIGHT.*

Questions 1-9.

DIRECTIONS: Questions 1 through 9 are to be answered SOLELY on the basis of the following information and the DIRECTORY OF SERVICES.

Officer Johnson has just been assigned to the North End Service Facility and is now on his post in the main lobby. The facility is open to the public from 9 A.M. to 5 P.M. each Monday through Friday, except on Thursdays when it is open from 9 A.M. to 7 P.M. The facility is closed on holidays.

Officer Johnson must ensure an orderly flow of visitors through the lobby of the facility. To accomplish this, Officer Johnson gives directions and provides routine information to clients and other members of the public who enter and leave the facility through the lobby.

In order to give directions and provide routine information to visitors, such as information concerning the location of services, Officer Johnson consults the Directory of Services shown below. Officer Johnson must ensure that clients are directed to the correct room for service and are sent to that room only during the hours that the particular service is available. When clients ask for the location of more than one service, they should be directed to go first to the service that will close soonest.

NORTH END SERVICE FACILITY
DIRECTORY OF SERVICES

Room	Type of Service	Days Available	Hours Open
101	Facility Receptionist	Monday, Tuesday, Wednesday, Friday Thursday	9 AM- 5 PM 9 AM- 7 PM
103	Photo Identification Cards	Monday, Wednesday, Friday	9 AM-12 Noon
104	Lost and Stolen Identification Cards	Wednesday, Thursday	9 AM-5 PM
105	Applications for Welfare/Food Stamps	Wednesday, Friday	1 PM-5 PM
107	Recertification for Welfare/Food Stamps	Monday, Thursday	10 AM- 12 Noon
108	Medicaid Applications	Tuesday, Wednesday	2 PM-5 PM
109	Medicaid Complaints	Tuesday, Wednesday	10 AM-2 PM
110, 111	Social Worker	Monday, Wednesday Tuesday, Friday Thursday	9 AM-12 Noon 1 PM-5 PM 9 AM- 5 PM
114	Hearing Room (By appointment only)	Monday, Thursday	9 AM-5 PM

DIRECTORY OF SERVICES
(CONT'D)

Room	Type of Service	Days Available	Hours Open
115	Hearing Information	Monday, Tuesday, Wednesday, Thursday, Friday	9 AM-1 PM
206, 207	Nutrition Aid	Monday, Wednesday, Friday Tuesday, Thursday	10 AM-2 PM 9 AM-12 Noon
215	Health Clinic	Monday, Tuesday, Wednesday, Friday Thursday	9 AM-5 PM 9 AM-7 PM
220	Facility Administrative Office	Monday, Tuesday, Wednesday, Thursday, Friday	9 AM-5 PM

1. It is Tuesday morning and Ms. Loretta Rogers, a client of the North End Service Facility, asks Officer Johnson where she should go in order to apply for Medicaid. Officer Johnson tells Ms. Rogers to go to Room _____ at _____.

    A. 108; 1:00 P.M.
    B. 109; 11:00 A.M.
    C. 108; 2:00 P.M.
    D. 109; 2:00 P.M.

2. On Friday at 11:00 A.M., Mrs. Ruth Ramos, a new client at the North End Service Facility, tells Officer Johnson that she wants to obtain a photo identification card and see a social worker.
   Officer Johnson should direct Mrs. Ramos to first go to Room

    A. 103   B. 104   C. 110   D. 220

3. On Friday at 10:30 A.M., a client at the North End Service Facility who is directed by Officer Johnson to go to Room 206 will be able to receive service regarding

    A. Recertification for Welfare/Food Stamps
    B. Hearing Information
    C. Medicaid Applications
    D. Nutrition Aid

4. At 9:00 A.M. on Monday, a client at the North End Service Facility who is directed by Officer Johnson to Room 101 for service will find

    A. Nutrition Aid
    B. Facility Receptionist
    C. Health Clinic
    D. Hearing Information

5. On Tuesday at 12:30 P.M., Mr. Paul Brown tells Officer Johnson that he lost his identification card and wants to obtain a new one as soon as possible.
   Officer Johnson should direct Mr. Brown to go to Room 104

    A. immediately
    B. at 1:00 P.M. that day
    C. at 9:00 A.M. on Wednesday
    D. at 2:00 P.M. on Friday

6. A client at the North End Service Facility explains to Officer Johnson that he wants to make an appointment with a Social Worker.
   The client should be directed to go to Room

   A. 104   B. 110   C. 115   D. 215

7. Ms. Alice Lee is a client at the North End Service Facility who has a 10:00 A.M. appointment on Thursday in the Hearing Room and does not know where to go.
   Officer Johnson should direct Ms. Lee to go to Room

   A. 101   B. 110   C. 112   D. 114

8. Officer Johnson is asked by a visitor which services are available on Thursdays between 5:00 P.M. and 7:00 P.M. Officer Johnson should inform the visitor that an available service during that time is

   A. Health Clinic
   B. Medicaid Complaints
   C. Nutrition Aid
   D. Social Worker

9. Mr. Jack Klein, a visitor to the North End Service Facility, asks Officer Johnson when and where he can file a complaint concerning Medicaid.
   Officer Johnson should inform Mr. Klein that he may go to Room

   A. 108 on Tuesday or Wednesday between 2:00 P.M. and 5:00 P.M.
   B. 109 on Tuesday or Wednesday between 10:00 A.M. and 2:00 P.M.
   C. 115 on Monday or Tuesday between 10:00 A.M. and 12:00 Noon
   D. 215 on Thursday between 9:00 A.M. and 7:00 P.M.

Questions 10-12.

DIRECTIONS: Questions 10 through 12 are to be answered SOLELY on the basis of the following information.

Security Officers should act in accordance with guidelines included in a manual provided to security staff. Assume that the following guidelines apply to Officers when in contact with visitors or clients in a facility:

1. Try to see things from the visitor's or client's point of view.
2. Ignore insulting comments.
3. Maintain a calm and patient manner.
4. Speak quietly, courteously, and tactfully.

10. Officer Renee Williams is patrolling the lobby area of her facility when she hears a client angrily yelling at the receptionist. She goes to investigate the situation and finds out from the receptionist that the client is one hour late for his appointment with a social worker who now has other appointments. The client demands to be seen by the social worker immediately. Officer Williams angrily tells the client that it is his own fault that he missed his appointment and he should stop bothering the receptionist and go home.
    In this situation, Officer Williams' behavior towards the client is

    A. *proper,* chiefly because it is the client's fault that he missed his appointment
    B. *improper,* chiefly because security officers should stay calm and speak courteously when dealing with clients
    C. *proper,* chiefly because the client had yelled at the receptionist
    D. *improper,* chiefly because the security officer should have ignored the whole incident

11. During his tour, Officer Montgomery is passing through his facility's waiting room on the way to the cafeteria for a break. As Officer Montgomery passes by a visitor, the visitor mutters an insulting remark about the Officer's appearance. Officer Montgomery ignores the visitor and the remark and proceeds on his way to the cafeteria.
Officer Montgomery's action in this situation is

   A. *correct,* chiefly because it is not necessary for Officer Montgomery to respond to visitors while on a break
   B. *incorrect,* chiefly because Officer Montgomery should have ejected the visitor from the facility
   C. *correct,* chiefly because special officers should ignore insults
   D. *incorrect,* chiefly because visitors should not be allowed to ridicule authority figures such as special officers

12. While patrolling the facility parking lot, Officer Klausner sees an unoccupied car parked in front of a fire hydrant. Officer Klausner writes out a summons for a parking violation and places it on the windshield of the car. As the Officer begins to walk away, the owner of the car spots the summons on the windshield and runs over to the car. The car owner is furious at getting the summons, confronts the Officer, and curses him loudly.
In this situation, Officer Klausner should

   A. curse back at the car owner just as loudly
   B. push him out of the way and resume patrol
   C. calmly explain to him the nature of the violation
   D. return all the insults but in a calm tone

Question 13.

DIRECTIONS: Question 13 is to be answered SOLELY on the basis of the following information.

Special Officers are permitted to give only general information about social services. They shall not provide advice concerning specific procedures.

13. Special Officer Lynn King is on post near the Medicaid Office in the Manhattan Income Maintenance Center. While Officer King is on post, a client approaches her and asks which forms must be filled out in order to apply for Medicaid benefits. Officer King tells the client that she cannot help him and directs the client to the Medicaid Office.
In this situation, Officer King's response to the client's question is

   A. *correct,* chiefly because Officer King's duties do not include providing any information to clients
   B. *incorrect,* chiefly because Officer King should have provided as much specific information as possible to the client
   C. *correct,* chiefly because Officer King may not advise clients on social services procedures
   D. *incorrect,* chiefly because Officer King should know which forms are used in the facility

Question 14.

DIRECTIONS: Question 14 is to be answered SOLELY on the basis of the following information.

Security Officers must request that visitors and clients show identification and inspect that identification before allowing them to enter restricted areas in the facility.

14. Security Officer Crane is assigned to a fixed post outside Commissioner Maxwell's office, which is a restricted area. A visitor approaches Officer Crane's desk and states that he is Robert Maxwell and has an appointment with the Commissioner, who is his brother. Officer Crane checks the appointment book, verifies that Robert Maxwell has an appointment with the Commissioner, and allows the visitor to enter the office.
In this situation, Officer Crane's action in allowing the visitor admittance to the Commissioner's office is

   A. *correct,* chiefly because he verified that Robert Maxwell had an appointment with the Commissioner
   B. *incorrect,* chiefly because all visitors must show identification before entering restricted areas
   C. *correct,* chiefly because it would insult the Commissioner's brother if he was asked to show identification
   D. *incorrect,* chiefly because he should have called the Commissioner to verify that he has a brother

Question 15.

DIRECTIONS: Question 15 is to be answered SOLELY on the basis of the following information.

While on duty, a Special Officer must give his rank, name, and shield number to any person who requests it.

15. Special Officer Karen Mitchell is assigned to patrol an area in the North Bronx Service Facility. While on patrol, Officer Mitchell observes a visitor asking other clients in the lobby for money. Upon investigation, she determines that the visitor has no official business in the facility and asks the visitor to leave the premises. The individual says that he will leave but demands to know Officer Mitchell's name and shield number.
In response to the visitor's demand, Officer Mitchell should

   A. give the individual her name and shield number
   B. inform him that he can only obtain that information from her supervisor
   C. ignore his demand and resume her patrol
   D. tell the visitor that she will issue a summons to him if he keeps bothering her

Question 16.

DIRECTIONS: Question 16 is to be answered SOLELY on the basis of the following information.

A member of the Security Staff must follow guidelines for providing information to reporters concerning official facility business. Special Officers shall not be interviewed, nor make public speeches or statements pertaining to official business unless authorized. Security Staff must receive authorization from the Office of Public Affairs before speaking to reporters on any matters pertaining to official facility business.

16. You are a Special Officer in a Men's Shelter. A reporter approaches you as you are leaving the building. The reporter requests that you give an insider's view on conditions in the shelter. He assures you that you will remain anonymous.
You should tell the reporter that you

   A. must obtain permission from your immediate supervisor before giving any interviews
   B. will be more than happy to provide him with information concerning conditions in the shelter
   C. must receive authorization from the Office of Public Affairs before giving any interviews
   D. may not give him any information, but that your supervisor will be able to provide him with the requested information.

Questions 17-21.

DIRECTIONS: Questions 17 through 21 are to be answered SOLELY on the basis of the following information.

During their tours, Security Officers are required to transmit and receive information and commands over two-way portable radios from other security staff members. Officers use a numbered code to transmit information over the radio. For example, an officer who calls *10-13* into his radio communicates to other officers and supervisors that he is in need of assistance. Assume that the code numbers shown below along with their specified meanings are those used by Special Officers.

Code	Meaning
10-01	Call your command
10-02	Report to your command
10-03	Call Dispatcher
10-04	Acknowledgment
10-05	Repeat message
10-06	Stand-by
10-07	Verify
10-08	Respond to specified area and advise
10-10	Investigate
10-13	Officer needs help
10-20	Robbery in progress
10-21	Burglary in progress
10-22	Larceny in progress
10-24	Assault in progress
10-30	Robbery has occurred

10-31	Burglary has occurred
10-34	Assault has occurred
10-40	Unusual incident
10-41	Vehicle accident
10-42	Traffic or parking problem
10-43	Electrical problem
10-50	Dispute or noise
10-52	Disorderly person/group
10-60	Ambulance needed
10-61	Police Department assistance required
10-64	Fire alarm
10-70	Arrived at scene
10-71	Arrest
10-72	Unfounded
10-73	Condition corrected
10-74	Resuming normal duties

17. Officer Cramer is patrolling Parking Lot A when he receives a radio message from Sergeant Wong. Sergeant Wong directs Officer Cramer to respond to Parking Lot B to investigate a reported traffic problem. Upon arriving at Parking Lot B, Officer Cramer observes a vehicle blocking a loading dock so that a delivery truck cannot gain access to the dock. After notification is made to the owner of the vehicle, the vehicle is moved, allowing the delivery truck to gain access to the loading dock. Which of the following should Officer Cramer use to BEST report the events that occurred back to Sergeant Wong?   17.____

    A. 10-72, 10-41, 10-73   B. 10-70, 10-42, 10-73
    C. 10-70, 10-41, 10-74   D. 10-72, 10-42, 10-74

18. Officer Garret receives a message of *10-24, 10-10* on his radio from his supervisor, Sergeant Gomez. Officer Garret responds to the scene and later sends Sergeant Gomez the following message in response: *10-70, 10-72, 10-74*. Which of the following events are reported by use of those codes?
Sergeant Gomez ordered Officer Garret to investigate an assault   18.____

    A. in progress. Officer Garret arrived at the scene, discovered that the report was unfounded, and resumed normal duties.
    B. that had occurred. Officer Garret arrived at the scene, made an arrest, and then resumed normal duties.
    C. that had occurred. Officer Garret arrived at the scene and discovered that the report was unfounded and resumed normal duties.
    D. in progress. Officer Garret arrived at the scene, made an arrest, and then resumed normal duties.

19. Officer Torres is patrolling the grounds of his facility when he receives a radio message from Sergeant Washington. In response to the radio message, Officer Torres goes to the facility's parking lot and issues a summons to a vehicle blocking an ambulance entrance. The radio message that Officer Torres received from Sergeant Washington is 10-10,

   A. 10-21   B. 10-40   C. 10-42   D. 10-43

20. Officer Oxford transmits the following codes by radio to Sergeant Joseph: *10-20, 10-13*. The response that Officer Oxford receives from Sergeant Joseph on her radio is *10-04*. Which one of the following events are reported by the use of those codes?
    Officer Oxford informed Sergeant Joseph that

   A. a robbery was in progress and that she needs assistance, and Sergeant Joseph acknowledged her message
   B. an assault was in progress and that she wants him to respond to the area, and Sergeant Joseph acknowledged her message
   C. a burglary was in progress and that someone must investigate, and Sergeant Joseph responded that he is standing by
   D. a larceny was in progress and that she needs him to call a dispatcher. Sergeant Joseph reports this incident to his command.

21. While on patrol, Officer Robinson observes that the hall lights in Wing *B* are flickering on and off. Officer Robinson calls the Maintenance Office and a maintenance worker responds and corrects the problem.
    The radio code that Officer Robinson should transmit to his supervisor to report this incident is

   A. 10-06,10-08   B. 10-40,10-64
   C. 10-43,10-73   D. 10-61,10-07

Question 22.

DIRECTIONS: Question 22 is to be answered SOLELY on the basis of the following information.

The two-way portable radios used by Security or Special Officers to communicate with other security staff members are to be used for official business only. In addition, when transmitting official business, transmission time (time spent transmitting information to other staff) should be kept to a minimum.

22. During his tour, Special Officer Banks calls Sergeant Gates in the patrolroom over the radio and asks if his wife, Alice Banks, had telephoned. Sergeant Gates tells Officer Banks that his wife has not called. Officer Banks then requests that Sergeant Gates notify him as soon as his wife calls because he is expecting an important message concerning his family.
    In this situation, Officer Banks' use of his radio is

   A. *appropriate,* chiefly because his transmission time was not excessive
   B. *inappropriate,* chiefly because he should have made the transmission on his break
   C. *appropriate,* chiefly because his transmission concerned an important family matter
   D. *inappropriate,* chiefly because radios are to be used for official business only

Question 23.

DIRECTIONS: Question 23 is to be answered SOLELY on the basis of the following information.

Special Officers are responsible for monitoring and responding to radio messages, even if the officer is on meal break, performing clerical duties, or away from his post for other reasons. An officer shall answer radio messages directed to him during his tour.

23. Officer Lewis is chatting with friends in the cafeteria while on her scheduled meal break when she receives a radio message from Sergeant Baker. Sergeant Baker informs Officer Lewis that trouble has broken out at Location A and directs her to report to Location A immediately to assist the officers on the scene. Officer Lewis leaves the cafeteria immediately and reports to the scene.
Officer Lewis' action in response to Sergeant Baker's radio message is

  A. *correct,* chiefly because Officer Lewis is responsible for responding to all radio messages
  B. *incorrect,* chiefly because Officer Lewis is on meal break and therefore *off-duty*
  C. *correct,* chiefly because Officer Lewis was not doing anything important during her meal break
  D. *incorrect,* chiefly because the situation was not declared a *total emergency*

Question 24.

DIRECTIONS: Question 24 is to be answered SOLELY on the basis of the following information.

Special Officers must immediately report to their supervisor any incident or condition in the facility that may cause danger or inconvenience to the public.

24. Special Officer Scott is patrolling a small, crowded waiting room in his facility when two male clients start arguing with each other, shoving chairs around and frightening the other clients. Officer Scott intervenes in the argument, issues summonses for Disorderly Conduct to the individuals involved in the dispute, and escorts them off the premises. Officer Scott then records the incident in his memo book and resumes patrol.
In this situation, the FIRST action that Officer Scott should have taken when he observed the argument start between the two men is to

  A. call for help from Special Officers on nearby posts to restrain the men who were fighting
  B. report the incident to his supervisor immediately
  C. attempt to separate the men who were fighting in order to stop the fight
  D. evacuate the waiting room so that innocent bystanders would not be injured

Question 25.

DIRECTIONS: Question 25 is to be answered SOLELY on the basis of the following information.

An Officer on duty in a facility must remain on post until properly relieved. If not properly relieved as scheduled, he must notify his immediate supervisor by radio of this fact and follow the supervisor's instructions.

25. Officer Clough is working on an 8:00 A.M. to 4:00 P.M. tour. Officer Clough is to be relieved at 4:00 P.M. by Security Officer Crandall, who works the 4:00 P.M. to 12:00 Midnight shift. However, as of 4:15 P.M., Officer Crandall has not appeared to relieve Officer Clough, so Officer Clough leaves his post to find Officer Crandall. In this situation, Officer Clough's action is

    A. *correct,* chiefly because his tour was over and he wanted to go home
    B. *incorrect,* chiefly because he should have notified his supervisor of Officer Crandall's failure to relieve him
    C. *correct,* chiefly because Officer Clough is attempting to locate Officer Crandall so that the post will be covered
    D. *incorrect,* chiefly because Officer Clough should have left his post as soon as his tour ended rather than working any overtime

Questions 26-28.

DIRECTIONS: Questions 26 through 28 are to be answered SOLELY on the basis of the following information.

A summons is a written notice that a person is accused of violating a code or regulation. Special Officers have the authority to issue summonses to individuals for on-premises parking or traffic violations, or violations of the City Administrative Code. Summonses for violations of the Penal Law, such as for Disorderly Conduct, may also be issued.

The following is a list of types of summonses issued for violations and their descriptions:

Type of Summons	Description of Violation
Class A	Parking in fire lanes
Class A	Parking in space reserved for the handicapped
Class A	Vehicle blocking driveway
Class B	Disobeying stop sign
Class C	Disorderly Conduct
Class C	Harassment
Environmental Control Board	Smoking Violations
Environmental Control Board	Public Health Code

26. While on patrol, Special Officer Gladys Jones observes a parked car that is blocking a driveway.
She should issue a summons for a violation which is a

    A. Class A type   B. Class B type
    C. Class C type   D. Environmental Control Board

27. A man drives up to a facility, parks his car in a fire lane, and quickly runs inside the facility. An attempt to follow and locate the man is unsuccessful.
Which one of the following is the type of summons that the Special Officer on duty should issue?

    A. Class A
    B. Class B
    C. Class C
    D. Environmental Control Board

28. While on patrol, Special Officer Mason observes a visitor smoking a cigarette in an area where smoking is prohibited. Officer Mason asks the visitor to stop smoking and shows him the *No Smoking* sign posted. The visitor refuses to comply.
Officer Mason should issue which type of summons?

    A. Class A
    B. Class B
    C. Class C
    D. Environmental Control Board

Questions 29-31.

DIRECTIONS: Questions 29 through 31 are to be answered SOLELY on the basis of the following information and the Summons Form and Fact Pattern.

Special Officers must complete a summons form by filling in the appropriate information. A completed summons must include the name and address of the accused; license or other identification number; vehicle identification; the section number of the code, regulation, or law violated; a brief description of the violation; any scheduled fine; information about the time and place of occurrence; and the name, rank, and signature of the Special Officer issuing the summons.

The information listed on the Summons Form may or may not be correct.

SUMMONS FORM

LINE			
	NOTICE OF VIOLATION No. 5 56784989	THE PEOPLE OF THE STATE OF NEW YORK VS.	
1		OPERATOR PRESENT NO (YES) REFUSED ID	
2	LAST NAME *Tucker*	FIRST NAME *James*	MIDDLE INITIAL *T*
3	STREET ADDRESS *205 E. 53rd Street*		
4	CITY (AS SHOWN ON LICENSE) *Brooklyn, NY 11234*		
5	DRIVER LICENSE OR IDENTIFICATION NO. *J-7156907834*	STATE *NY*	CLASS *5* DATE EXPIRES *1/12/13*
6	SEX *M*	DATE OF BIRTH *1/12/65*	
7	LICENSE PLATE NO. *CVR-632* STATE *NY* DATE EXPIRES *8/12/12*		OPERATOR OWN VEHICLE? (YES) NO
8	BODY TYPE *Sedan*	MAKE *Dodge*	COLOR *Green*
	THE PERSON DESCRIBED ABOVE IS CHARGED AS FOLLOWS:		
9	ISSUE TIME *9:30 A.M.* DATE OF OFFENSE *2/5/12*	TIME FIRST OBSERVED *9:28 A.M.*	COUNTY *Kings*
10	PLACE OF OCCURRENCE *451 Clarkson Ave., Brooklyn, NY*		PRECINCT *71st*
11	IN VIOLATION OF SECTION *81-B* CODE *40* LAW *New York State Traffic Regulation*		
12	DESCRIPTION OF VIOLATION *Vehicle parked in front of a fire hydrant*		
13	SCHEDULED FINE $10 $15 $20 $25 $30 ($40) Other $____		
14	RANK/NAME OF ISSUING OFFICER *Special Officer Joseph Robbins*	SIGNATURE OF ISSUING OFFICER *Joseph Robbins*	

FACT PATTERN

On February 5, 2012, at 9:28 A.M., Special Officer Joseph Robbins is patrolling the grounds of the Brooklyn Hills Income Maintenance Center, located at 451 Clarkson Ave., Brooklyn, NY, when he observes an unoccupied parked vehicle blocking a fire hydrant near the facility's entrance. As Officer Robbins begins to write up a summons for the violation, James Tucker, the owner of the vehicle, emerges from the facility and comes over. While getting in his car, he asks why he is getting a summons. Officer Robbins explains to Mr. Tucker that he is in violation of traffic regulations pertaining to access to fire hydrants and asks him for identification. Mr. Tucker gives Officer Robbins his driver's license, showing the following information:

Name:	Tucker, James T.
Address:	205 E. 53rd Street, Brooklyn, NY 11234
Date of Birth:	January 12, 1965
Driver's License:	J-7156907894
Driver License Expiration Date:	January 12, 2013
Class:	5

29. The *place of occurrence* of the violation described in the Fact Pattern is on line _____ of the Summons Form.

    A. 2   B. 3   C. 8   D. 10

30. Which one of the following lines on the Summons Form shows information that does NOT agree with information given in the Fact Pattern?

    A. 1   B. 2   C. 4   D. 5

31. Which of the following is the date on which the violation occurred?

    A. 1/12/12   B. 2/5/12   C. 8/12/12   D. 1/12/13

32. Following are two sentences which may or may not be written in correct English:
    I. Two clients assaulted the officer.
    II. The van is illegally parked.

    Which one of the following statements is CORRECT?

    A. Only Sentence I is written in correct English.
    B. Only Sentence II is written in correct English.
    C. Sentences I and II are both written in correct English.
    D. Neither Sentence I nor Sentence II is written in correct English.

33. Following are two sentences which may or may not be written in correct English:
    I. Security Officer Rollo escorted the visitor to the patrolroom.
    II. Two entry were made in the facility logbook.

    Which one of the following statements is CORRECT?

    A. Only Sentence I is written in correct English.
    B. Only Sentence II is written in correct English.
    C. Sentences I and II are both written in correct English.
    D. Neither Sentence I nor Sentence II is written in correct English.

34. Following are two sentences which may or may not be written in correct English:
    I. Officer McElroy putted out a small fire in the wastepaper basket.
    II. Special Officer Janssen told the visitor where he could obtained a pass.
Which one of the following statements is CORRECT?

   A. Only Sentence I is written in correct English.
   B. Only Sentence II is written in correct English.
   C. Sentences I and II are both written in correct English.
   D. Neither Sentence I nor Sentence II are written in correct English.

35. Following are two sentences which may or may not be written in correct English:
    I. Security Officer Warren observed a broken window while he was on his post in Hallway C.
    II. The worker reported that two typewriters had been stoled from the office.
Which one of the following statements is CORRECT?

   A. Only Sentence I is written in correct English.
   B. Only Sentence II is written in correct English.
   C. Sentences I and II are both written in correct English.
   D. Neither Sentence I nor Sentence II is written in correct English.

KEY (CORRECT ANSWERS)

1.	C	16.	C
2.	A	17.	B
3.	D	18.	A
4.	B	19.	C
5.	C	20.	A
6.	B	21.	C
7.	D	22.	D
8.	A	23.	A
9.	B	24.	B
10.	B	25.	B
11.	C	26.	A
12.	C	27.	A
13.	C	28.	D
14.	B	29.	D
15.	A	30.	D

31. B
32. C
33. A
34. D
35. A

TEST 2

DIRECTIONS: Each question or incomplete statement is followed by several suggested answers or completions. Select the one that BEST answers the question or completes the statement. *PRINT THE LETTER OF THE CORRECT ANSWER IN THE SPACE AT THE RIGHT.*

Questions 1-5.

DIRECTIONS: Questions 1 through 5 are to be answered SOLELY on the basis of the following information.

Special Officers have the power to arrest members of the public who commit crimes in violation of the Penal Law. Assume that certain classes of crimes covered by various sections of the Penal Law are described below. Special Officers must be able to apply this information when making an arrest in order to accurately determine the type of crime that has been committed.

Crime	Class of Crime	Description of Crime	Section
Petit Larceny	A Misdemeanor	Stealing property worth up to $250	155.25
Grand Larceny 3rd Degree	E Felony	Stealing property worth more than $250	155.30
Grand Larceny 2nd Degree	D Felony	Stealing property worth more than $1,500	155.35
Grand Larceny 1st Degree	C Felony	Stealing property worth any amount of money while making a person fear injury or damage to property	155.40
Assault 3rd Degree	A Misdemeanor	Injuring a person	120.00
Assault 2nd Degree	D Felony	1. Seriously injuring a person; or 2. Injuring an officer of the law	120.05
Assault 1st Degree	C Felony	Seriously injuring a person using a deadly or dangerous weapon	120.10
Disorderly Conduct	Violation	1. Engages in fighting or threatening behavior; or 2. Makes unreasonable noise	240.20
Robbery 3rd Degree	D Felony	Stealing property by force	160.05
Robbery 2nd Degree	C Felony	1. Stealing property by force with the help of another person; or 2. Stealing property by force and injuring any person	160.10
Robbery 1st Degree	B Felony	Stealing property by force and seriously injuring the owner of property	160.15

1. Which one of the following crimes is considered to be Class A Misdemeanor?

   A. Grand Larceny - 3rd Degree
   B. Grand Larceny - 2nd Degree
   C. Assault - 3rd Degree
   D. Assault - 2nd Degree

2. Which one of the following crimes is considered to be Class B Felony?

   A. Robbery - 2nd Degree
   B. Robbery - 1st Degree
   C. Grand Larceny - 3rd Degree
   D. Grand Larceny - 2nd Degree

3. A worker at a facility reports that a typewriter worth $400 has been stolen from her office. Which one of the following is the type of crime that has been committed?

   A. Grand Larceny - 3rd Degree
   B. Grand Larceny - 2nd Degree
   C. Grand Larceny - 1st Degree
   D. Petit Larceny

4. A visitor at a facility begins yelling very loudly at a receptionist and shakes his fist at her. The visitor refuses to stop yelling when an officer tries to calm him down, and he shakes his fist at the officer. Which one of the following is the type of crime that occurred?

   A. Assault - 3rd Degree
   B. Assault - 2nd Degree
   C. Assault - 1st Degree
   D. Disorderly Conduct

5. An officer has apprehended and arrested a visitor who was attempting to leave the facility with a radio he had stolen from an office. The radio is worth $100.
   Under which one of the following sections of the Penal Law should the visitor be charged? Section

   A. 155.25   B. 155.30   C. 155.35   D. 155.40

Questions 6-12.

DIRECTIONS: Questions 6 through 12 are to be answered SOLELY on the basis of the Arrest Report Form and Incident Report shown on the following page. These reports were submitted by Special Officer John Clark, Shield #512, to his supervisor, Sergeant Joseph Lewis, Shield #818, of the North Bay Health Clinic

Special Officers are required to complete both an Arrest Report Form and an Incident Report whenever an unusual incident or an arrest occurs. The Arrest Report Form provides detailed information regarding the victim and the person arrested, along with a brief description of the incident.

The Incident Report provides a detailed description of the incident. Both reports include the following information: WHO was involved in the incident, including witnesses; WHAT happened and HOW it happened; WHERE and WHEN the incident occurred; and WHY the incident occurred.

ARREST REPORT FORM

ARREST INFORMATION (1)	TIME OF OCCURRENCE 11:15 A.M.	DATE OF OCCURRENCE February 1, 2012	DAY OF WEEK Monday	
INFORMATION ABOUT VICTIM (2)	VICTIM'S NAME Darlene Kirk		ADDRESS 7855 Cruger St., Bronx, NY 10488	
(3)	SEX F	DATE OF BIRTH 9/3/75	RACE White	HOME TELEPHONE # 212-733-3462	SOCIAL SECURITY # 245-63-0772
INFORMATION ABOUT PERSON ARRESTED (4)	NAME OF PERSON ARRESTED Elsie Gardner		ADDRESS 2447 Southern Pkway, Bronx, NY 10467	
(5)	SEX F	DATE OF BIRTH 7/9/80	RACE White	HOME TELEPHONE # 212-513-7029	SOCIAL SECURITY # 244-08-0569
(6)	HEIGHT 5'5"	WEIGHT 135 lbs.	HAIR COLOR Brown	CLOTHING Black coat/red pants	
DESCRIPTION OF CRIME (7)	SECTION OF PENAL LAW 120.00		TYPE OF CRIME Assault - 3rd Degree	
(8)	TIME OF ARREST 11:35 A.M.	DATE OF ARREST 2/1/12	LOCATION OF ARREST 635 Bay Avenue Bronx, NY	
(9)	DESCRIPTION OF INCIDENT The defendant, Elsie Gardner, struck the victim after the victim requested that Ms. Gardner stop smoking in a "NO SMOKING" area. Two witnesses verified the victim's account of the incident.			
INFORMATION ABOUT ARRESTING OFFICER (10)	REPORTING OFFICER'S SIGNATURE *John Clark*		NAME PRINTED John Clark	
(11)	RANK Special Officer		SHIELD NUMBER 512	

INCIDENT REPORT

(1) At 11:15 A.M. on February 1, 2012, I was directed by Sergeant Mark Lewis via two-way radio to report to the Nutrition Clinic on the 4th Floor to investigate a disturbance. (2) Special Officer Anna Colon, Shield #433, was directed to assist me. (3) At 11:16 A.M., Officer Colon and I arrived at the Health Clinic and observed a patient, Elsie Gardner, repeatedly strike Health Clinic receptionist Darlene Kirk about the head and neck. (4) Officer Colon restrained Ms. Gardner while I placed handcuffs on her wrists. (5) Ms. Kirk complained that her neck felt sore. (6) After being examined by Dr. Stone, Ms. Kirk told us that Ms. Gardner entered the Health Clinic at approximately 11:10 A.M. and lit a cigarette in the waiting area. (7) At 11:20 A.M., Dr. Paul Stone examined Ms. Kirk. (8) Ms. Kirk explained to Ms. Gardner that smoking was not allowed in the Health Clinic and showed her the NO SMOKING signs posted on the walls. (9) Ms. Gardner ignored Ms. Kirk, and then grew very abusive and attacked her when Ms. Kirk insisted that she stop smoking. (10) Two witnesses, patients Edna Manning of 8937 4th Ave., Bronx, NY, and John Schultz of 357 149th Street, Bronx, NY, gave the same account of the incident as Ms. Kirk. (11) At 11:30 A.M., I read the prisoner her rights and placed her under arrest for violation of Penal Law Section 120.00 -Assault 3rd Degree. (12) At 11:35 A.M., I notified the 86th Precinct of Ms. Gardner's arrest and arranged for the transportation of the prisoner to the precinct. (13) At 11:40 A.M., Officer Colon escorted Ms. Gardner from the Nutrition Clinic to the patrolroom. (14) At 11:55 A.M., Police Officers Cranford, Shield #658, and Wargo, Shield #313, arrived at the facility to transport the prisoner to the precinct. (15) Officer Gray, Shield #936, assumed my post while I reported to the patrolroom to complete the necessary forms concerning the arrest.

6. At what time did Sergeant Lewis inform Officer John Clark of the disturbance in the Nutrition Clinic?
   _____ A.M.

   A. 11:00   B. 11:15   C. 11:16   D. 11:20

7. According to the Arrest Report and the Incident Report, how many witnesses gave the same account of the incident as Ms. Kirk?

   A. 1   B. 2   C. 3   D. 4

8. What information on the Arrest Report is NOT included in the Incident Report?

   A. Date of Occurrence
   B. Victim's address
   C. Section of the Penal Law violated
   D. Assault 3rd Degree

9. Which sentence in the Incident Report is out of order in terms of the sequence of events?

   A. 3   B. 6   C. 11   D. 12

10. According to the Incident Report, at 11:40 A.M. Ms. Gardner was

    A. escorted to the patrolroom
    B. transported to the 86th Precinct
    C. examined by Dr. Paul Stone
    D. giving an account of the incident to Special Officers Clark and Colon

11. According to the Incident Report, which one of the following officers relieved Officer Clark?
    Officer

    A. Colon   B. Cranford   C. Wargo   D. Gray

12. Which section of the Arrest Report contains information that does NOT agree with Sentence 11 of the Incident Report?
    Section

    A. 1   B. 7   C. 8   D. 9

Question 13.

DIRECTIONS: Question 13 is to be answered SOLELY on the basis of the following information.

A Security Officer must investigate any complaint or incident which occurs in the facility, whether he considers it is major or minor. The Officer must also interview the person(s) involved in the incident in order to complete the necessary forms and reports.

13. Ms. Peters, a clerical worker at the facility, complains to Officer Tynan that a pen set, which had been given to her as a gift, was missing from her desk. She tells Officer Tynan that she knows the pen set was on her desk the previous day because she was using it for her work. Officer Tynan informs Ms. Peters that there is nothing he can do since the pen set was personal property and not facility property.
In this situation, Officer Tynan's response to Ms. Peters is

   A. *correct,* chiefly because the pen set should not have been left out on a desk where it could be stolen
   B. *incorrect,* chiefly because a complaint of a loss of theft should be investigated and recorded
   C. *correct,* chiefly because Special Officers are only required to investigate a loss or theft of facility property
   D. *incorrect,* chiefly because Ms. Peters' work required use of the pen set

Question 14.

DIRECTIONS: Question 14 is to be answered SOLELY on the basis of the following information.

Assume that Security Officers are responsible for recording in a personal memobook all of their routine and non-routine activities and occurrences for each tour of duty. Before starting a tour of duty, a Security Officer must enter in his personal memobook the date, tour, and assigned post. An entry shall be made to record each absence from duty, such as a regular day off, sick leave, annual leave, or holiday. During each tour, a Security Officer shall enter a full and accurate record of duties performed, changes in post assignment, absences from post, and the reason for each absence, and all other patrol business.

14. Security Officer Ella Lewis is assigned to Gotham Center Facility, where she works Monday through Friday on a 9:00 A.M. to 5:00 P.M. tour. Officer Lewis' regular days off are Saturday and Sunday. Officer Lewis worked on Wednesday, November 25, 2012. She was absent on Thursday, November 26, 2012, for Thanksgiving Holiday, and on Friday, November 27, 2012, for annual leave.
According to the information given above, which of the following entries is the FIRST entry that Officer Lewis should record in her memobook when she returns to work on November 30, 2012?

   A. Saturday, 11/28/12 and Sunday, 11/29/12 - Regular days off
   B. Friday, 11/27/12 - Sick Leave
   C. Monday, 11/30/12 - On duty
   D. Thursday, 11/26/12 - Thanksgiving Holiday

Questions 15-16.

DIRECTIONS: Questions 15 and 16 are to be answered SOLELY on the basis of the following entries recorded by Security Officer Angela Russo in her memobook.

Date: January 8, 2012
Tour: 8:00 A.M. to 4:00 P.M.
Weather: Sunny and clear

6 (#2)

7:30	Reported to *B* Command for Roll Call. Assigned to Post #2, *C* Building Emergency Room Corridor by Sergeant Robert Floyd. Break: 9:30 A.M. Meal: 1:30 P.M. Radio: #701
7:40	Arrived at Post #2 and relieved Special Officer Johnson, Shield #593.
7:45	On patrol - Post #2.
8:00	Post #2 - All secure at this time; conditions normal.
8:30	Fire Alarm Box 5-3-1 rings on 3rd Floor South in *C* Building. Upon arrival, Office Worker Molly Lewis reported that a waste-paper basket was on fire. Used fire extinguisher to put out fire.
8:50	Condition corrected; Incident Report prepared and submitted to Sergeant Floyd in *B* Command.
8:55	Resumed patrol of Post #2.
9:30	Relieved for break by Officer Tucker.
9:50	Resumed patrol of Post #2.
10:10	Disorderly person reported by Clinic Director Lila Jones on Ward C-32; Officer Bailey and myself responded. Clinic Director Jones informed officers that visitor Bradley Manna, male white, 19 years of age, 2 Park Place, Brooklyn, NY, is drunk and has been shouting insults to Clinic staff.
10:30	Condition corrected; Visitor Bradley Manna escorted off premises. *B* Command notified of incident.
10:40	Resumed patrol of Post #2.
11:40	Post #2 - All secure at this time.
12:40	Post #2 - All secure at this time.

15. The name of the Clinic Director who reported a disorderly person is   15.____

    A. Molly Lewis   B. Bradley Manna
    C. Lila Jones   D. Robert Floyd

16. Which of the following sets of officers responded to the report of a disorderly person on Ward C-32?   16.____
Officers

    A. Johnson and Bailey   B. Russo and Tucker
    C. Johnson and Tucker   D. Russo and Bailey

17. Security Officer Mace is completing an entry in her memo-book. The entry has the following five sentences:
    1. I observed the defendant removing a radio from a facility vehicle.
    2. I placed the defendant under arrest and escorted him to the patrolroom.
    3. I was patrolling the facility parking lot.
    4. I asked the defendant to show identification.
    5. I determined that the defendant was not authorized to remove the radio.
    The MOST logical order for these sentences to be entered in Officer Mace's memo-book is

    A. 1, 3, 2, 4, 5
    B. 2, 5, 4, 1, 3
    C. 3, 1, 4, 5, 2
    D. 4, 5, 2, 1, 3

18. Security Officer Riley is completing an entry in his memo-book. The entry has the following five sentences:
    1. Anna Jones admitted that she stole Mary Green's wallet.
    2. I approached the women and asked them who they were and why they were arguing.
    3. I arrested Anna Jones for stealing Mary Green's wallet.
    4. They identified themselves and Mary Green accused Anna Jones of stealing her wallet.
    5. I was in the lobby area when I observed two women arguing about a wallet.
    The MOST logical order for these sentences to be entered in Officer Riley's memobook is

    A. 2, 4, 1, 3, 5
    B. 3, 1, 4, 5, 2
    C. 4, 1, 5, 2, 3
    D. 5, 2, 4, 1, 3

19. Assume that Security Officer John Ryan is completing an entry in his memobook. The entry has the following five sentences:
    1. I then cleared the immediate area of visitors and staff.
    2. I noticed smoke coming from a broom closet outside Room A71.
    3. Sergeant Mueller arrived with other officers to assist in clearing the area.
    4. Upon investigation, I determined the smoke was due to burning material in the broom closet.
    5. I pulled the corridor fire alarm and notified Sergeant Mueller of the fire.
    The MOST logical order for these sentences to be entered in Officer Ryan's memo-book is

    A. 2, 3, 4, 5, 1
    B. 2, 4, 5, 1, 3
    C. 4, 1, 2, 3, 5
    D. 5, 3, 2, 1, 4

20. Security Officer Hernandez is completing an entry in his memobook. The entry has the following five sentences:
    1. I asked him to leave the premises immediately.
    2. A visitor complained that there was a strange man loitering in Clinic B hallway.
    3. I went to investigate and saw a man dressed in rags sitting on the floor of the hallway.
    4. As he walked out, he started yelling that he had no place to go.
    5. I asked to see identification, but he said that he did not have any.
    The MOST logical order for these sentences to be entered in Officer Hernandez's memobook is

A.	2, 3, 5, 1, 4	B.	3, 1, 2, 4, 5
C.	4, 1, 5, 2, 3	D.	3, 1, 5, 2, 4

21. Officer Hogan is completing an entry in his memobook. The entry has the following five sentences: 21._____
    1. When the fighting had stopped, I transmitted a message requesting medical assistance for Mr. Perkins.
    2. Special Officer Manning assisted me in stopping the fight.
    3. When I arrived at the scene, I saw a client, Adam Finley strike a facility employee, Peter Perkins.
    4. As I attempted to break up the fight, Special Officer Manning came on the scene.
    5. I received a radio message from Sergeant Valez to investigate a possible fight in progress in the waiting room.

    The MOST logical order for these sentences to be entered in Officer Hogan's memobook is

A.	2, 1, 4, 5, 3	B.	3, 5, 2, 4, 1
C.	4, 5, 3, 1, 2	D.	5, 3, 4, 2, 1

Questions 22-23.

DIRECTIONS: Questions 22 and 23 are to be answered SOLELY on the basis of the following information.

Assume that Security Officers may be assigned to the facility patrolroom and must follow the guidelines below in documenting all routine and non-routine activities and occurrences in the facility logbook.

At the beginning of each tour of duty, the Security Officer responsible for entering information in the logbook must transfer from the Roll Call Sheet to the logbook a list of all security staff personnel assigned to that tour. This list is to be entered in order of the rank of the security staff member. All other entries in the facility logbook shall be recorded in chronological order, in blue or black ink, and be neat and legible.

22. When recording the list of security staff personnel assigned to a tour, that entry shall be made in   22._____

    A. chronological order
    B. order of rank of security staff
    C. alphabetical order
    D. order of arrival at facility

23. A Security Officer has transmitted notification to the patrolroom that he has just issued a summons. The Security Officer responsible for documenting occurrences in the patrolroom logbook should record the information   23._____

    A. in red ink, immediately following the previous entry
    B. on a new page under the heading *Summonses Reported*
    C. in blue or black ink immediately following the previous entry
    D. on the last page of the logbook where it can be easily found

Question 24.

DIRECTIONS: Question 24 is to be answered SOLELY on the basis of the following information.

Assume that whenever a Security Officer is to begin a leave of absence, long-term sick leave, or other type of leave having an anticipated length of ten days or more, the officer shall surrender his or her security shield to his supervisor, who shall immediately forward it to Security Headquarters.

24. Two male clients were fighting in the waiting room of North End Hospital. Officer Gary Klott attempted to separate them and became involved in the altercation. Officer Klott sustained an injury to the right eye and was examined by a physician. The physician directed Officer Klott to stay home for a recovery period of 12 days. In this situation, Officer Klott should

    A. surrender his shield to his supervisor
    B. safeguard his shield in a safe place at home while he is recovering
    C. surrender his shield to the physician
    D. safeguard his shield with his uniform in his locker at the facility while he is recovering

Question 25.

DIRECTIONS: Question 25 is to be answered SOLELY on the basis of the following information.

Assume that Security Officers are required to follow certain procedures when on post at a restricted area of a facility. They must inspect the identification of employees and passes of visitors, as well as all bags and packages carried by individuals who wish to enter the restricted area.

25. Security Officer Stevens is assigned to a post at the Intensive Care Unit of Park View Hospital, a restricted area. Officer Stevens is responsible for inspecting identification and passes, as well as all bags and packages carried by individuals who want to enter the Unit. He sees Mr. Craig approach. He knows Mr. Craig's wife is a patient in the Unit. Officer Stevens has seen Mr. Craig visit his wife every day for the past four days. Mr. Craig brings a small duffel bag filled with magazines each time he comes. Today, Officer Stevens checks Mr. Craig's visitor's pass but lets Mr. Craig enter the Unit without checking his duffel bag. In this situation, Officer Stevens' action is

    A. *correct,* chiefly because he has checked to see that Mr. Craig has a visitor's pass
    B. *incorrect,* chiefly because all packages and bags must be inspected before anyone is allowed to enter a restricted area
    C. *correct,* chiefly because he is familiar with Mr. Craig and knows that he only carries magazines in his duffel bag
    D. *incorrect,* chiefly because Mr. Craig should not be allowed to carry a bag or package into a restricted area of the facility

Question 26.

DIRECTIONS: Question 26 is to be answered SOLELY on the basis of the following information.

Assume that Special Officers must safeguard evidence in cases involving firearms. Special Officers must mark recovered bullets for identification purposes. The Officer who recovers the bullet must mark his or her initials and the date of recovery of the bullet on the base or on the nose of the bullet.

26. On January 18, 2012, at 11:30 P.M., an unidentified person fired a shot at an unoccupied security patrol car in the facility parking lot. Officer Debra Johnson was assigned to investigate the matter. A fired bullet was recovered inside the patrol car by Officer Johnson at 1:00 A.M. on January 19, 2012.
Officer Johnson should mark *D.J. 1/19/12* on

    A. the base or the nose of the recovered bullet
    B. the side of the recovered bullet
    C. an envelope and place the recovered bullet inside
    D. the side of the patrol car from which the bullet was recovered

Question 27.

DIRECTIONS: Question 27 is to be answered SOLELY on the basis of the following information.

Patrolroom Observers are officers who are assigned to observe events when individuals, other than security staff, are present in the patrolroom. According to facility guidelines, a Patrolroom Observer must be called to the patrolroom to serve as a witness whenever any individual is brought to the patrolroom for any reason by a Special Officer.

27. Janet Childs, a client at Gotham Health Facility, was robbed in the facility's parking lot. Ms. Childs was not harmed as a result of the incident, but she was upset. Special Officer Grey escorted her to the patrol-room, where she remained until she felt better. While she was waiting in the patrolroom, Officer Grey did not call a Patrolman Observer to the patrolroom during the time that Ms. Childs was there.
In this situation, Officer Grey

    A. should not have taken Ms. Childs to the patrolroom without special authorization from his supervisor
    B. was not required to call a Patrolroom Observer to the patrolroom since Ms. Childs had not been placed under arrest
    C. should have called a Patrolroom Observer to be present while Ms. Childs was in the patrolroom
    D. should have escorted Ms. Childs to the patrolroom and left her in the care of the Special Officer assigned to the patrolroom

Question 28.

DIRECTIONS: Question 28 is to be answered SOLELY on the basis of the following information.

Special Officers escort individuals categorized as Emotionally Disturbed Persons to the hospital for observation or treatment when directed to do so. These individuals are transported to the hospital by Emergency Medical Service (EMS) ambulance. There must be one Special Officer present in the ambulance for each Emotionally Disturbed Person transferred to the hospital, along with an EMS Technician and the ambulance driver.

28. Special Officers Patrick Lawson and Grace Martin have been assigned to escort two individuals categorized as Emotionally Disturbed Persons from that facility to a nearby hospital. The EMS ambulance, with an EMS Technician and ambulance driver, has arrived at the facility to transport the individuals. Officer Lawson then suggests to Officer Martin that it is not necessary for him to go to the hospital since the EMS Technician will be with Officer Martin in the ambulance.
In this situation, Officer Lawson's suggestion is

    A. *correct,* since an EMS Technician will be present in the ambulance to accompany Officer Martin and the Emotionally Disturbed Persons to the hospital
    B. *incorrect,* since one Special Officer must be present in the ambulance for each Emotionally Disturbed Person transported to the hospital
    C. *correct,* since the Emotionally Disturbed Persons are unlikely to cause any disturbance inside the ambulance
    D. *incorrect,* since two EMS Technicians must be present in the ambulance when only one Special Officer is escorting two Emotionally Disturbed Persons to the hospital

28.____

Questions 29-32.

DIRECTIONS: Questions 29 through 32 are to be answered on the basis of the following information.

Assume that information concerning new or updated policies and procedures are sometimes provided to facility security staff in the form of a memorandum from Security Headquarters.

Question 29.

DIRECTIONS: Question 29 is to be answered SOLELY on the basis of the following memorandum.

TO: All Security Officers
FROM: Security Headquarters
SUBJECT: Smoking Regulations

At times, Security Officers have been observed smoking while on duty at their assigned posts. This is strictly prohibited. If Officers feel that they must smoke, they may smoke during breaks or lunch period in designated areas. Officers may not smoke while on official duty. If any Officer is observed smoking while on post or while performing official duties, appropriate disciplinary action will be taken.

29. According to the above memorandum, Security Officers may

 A. smoke while on duty, as long as they are out of view of the public
 B. not smoke while on duty except when assigned to a post in a designated smoking area
 C. smoke on breaks or during lunch period in designated areas
 D. not smoke at any time when dressed in official uniform

Question 30.

DIRECTIONS: Question 30 is to be answered SOLELY on the basis of the following memorandum.

TO: All Special Officers
FROM: Security Headquarters
SUBJECT: Safeguarding Shields and Identification Cards

Special Officers must ensure that their shields and identification cards are secure at all times. Should an officer become aware of the loss or theft of his shield or identification card, he shall immediately report such loss or theft to Security Headquarters.

30. According to the above memorandum, a Special Officer must

 A. report the loss or theft of his identification card to the nearest police precinct
 B. secure his shield in his locker at all times
 C. report the loss or theft of his shield or identification card to Security Headquarters immediately
 D. secure his identification card at Security Headquarters each night before leaving the facility

Question 31.

DIRECTIONS: Question 31 is to be answered SOLELY on the basis of the following memorandum.

TO: All Security Officers
FROM: Security Headquarters
SUBJECT: Fire in the Facility

Special Officers must report immediately to assist at the scene of a fire when directed to do so by a supervisor. Officers shall remain at the scene and ensure that only authorized personnel are in an area restricted by a fire emergency. Visitors and clients shall be directed to the nearest safe stairwell and out of the facility. Visitors and clients are not to use elevators to evacuate the area.

31. According to the above memorandum, a Security Officer should

 A. direct visitors and clients to the nearest elevator in case of fire
 B. report unauthorized personnel at a fire scene to the Fire Department
 C. escort visitors and clients down the nearest stairwell and out of the facility
 D. ensure that only authorized personnel are in an area restricted by a fire emergency

13 (#2)

Question 32.

DIRECTIONS: Question 32 is to be answered SOLELY on the basis of the following memorandum.

TO: All Security Officers
FROM: Security Headquarters
SUBJECT: Reporting Unsafe Conditions

Security Officers shall report to their supervisors and appropriate facility staff any condition that could affect the safety or security of the facility. Conditions such as broken windows, unlocked doors and water leaks should be reported.

32. According to the above memorandum, a Security Officer shall   32._____

    A. make recommendations to his superiors concerning other facility staff members
    B. correct all unsafe conditions such as broken windows
    C. report a condition such as a water leak to his supervisor and appropriate facility staff
    D. make recommendations to facility staff concerning doors to be left unlocked

33. Following are two sentences that may or may not be written in correct English: 33._____
    I. Special Officer Cleveland was attempting to calm an emotionally disturbed visitor.
    II. The visitor did not stops crying and calling for his wife.
Which one of the following statements is CORRECT?

    A. Only Sentence I is written in correct English.
    B. Only Sentence II is written in correct English.
    C. Sentences I and II are both written in correct English.
    D. Neither Sentence I nor Sentence II is written in correct English.

34. Following are two sentences that may or may not be written in correct English: 34._____
    I. While on patrol, I observes a vagrant loitering near the drug dispensary.
    II. I escorted the vagrant out of the building and off the premises.
Which one of the following statements is CORRECT?

    A. Only Sentence I is written in correct English.
    B. Only Sentence II is written in correct English.
    C. Sentences I and II are both written in correct English.
    D. Neither Sentence I nor Sentence II is written in correct English.

35. Following are two sentences that may or may not be written in correct English: 35._____
    I. At 4:00 P.M., Sergeant Raymond told me to evacuate the waiting area immediately due to a bomb threat.
    II. Some of the clients did not want to leave the building.
Which one of the following statements is CORRECT?

    A. Only Sentence I is written in correct English.
    B. Only Sentence II is written in correct English.
    C. Sentences I and II are both written in correct English.
    D. Neither Sentence I nor Sentence II is written in correct English.

KEY (CORRECT ANSWERS)

1.	C	16.	D
2.	B	17.	C
3.	A	18.	D
4.	D	19.	B
5.	A	20.	A
6.	B	21.	D
7.	B	22.	B
8.	B	23.	C
9.	B	24.	A
10.	A	25.	B
11.	D	26.	A
12.	C	27.	C
13.	B	28.	B
14.	D	29.	C
15.	C	30.	C

31. D
32. C
33. A
34. B
35. C

SCANNING MAPS

One section of the exam tests your ability to orient yourself within a given region on a map. Using the map accompanying questions 1 through 3; choose the best way of getting from one point to another.

The New Bridge is closed to traffic because it has a broken span.

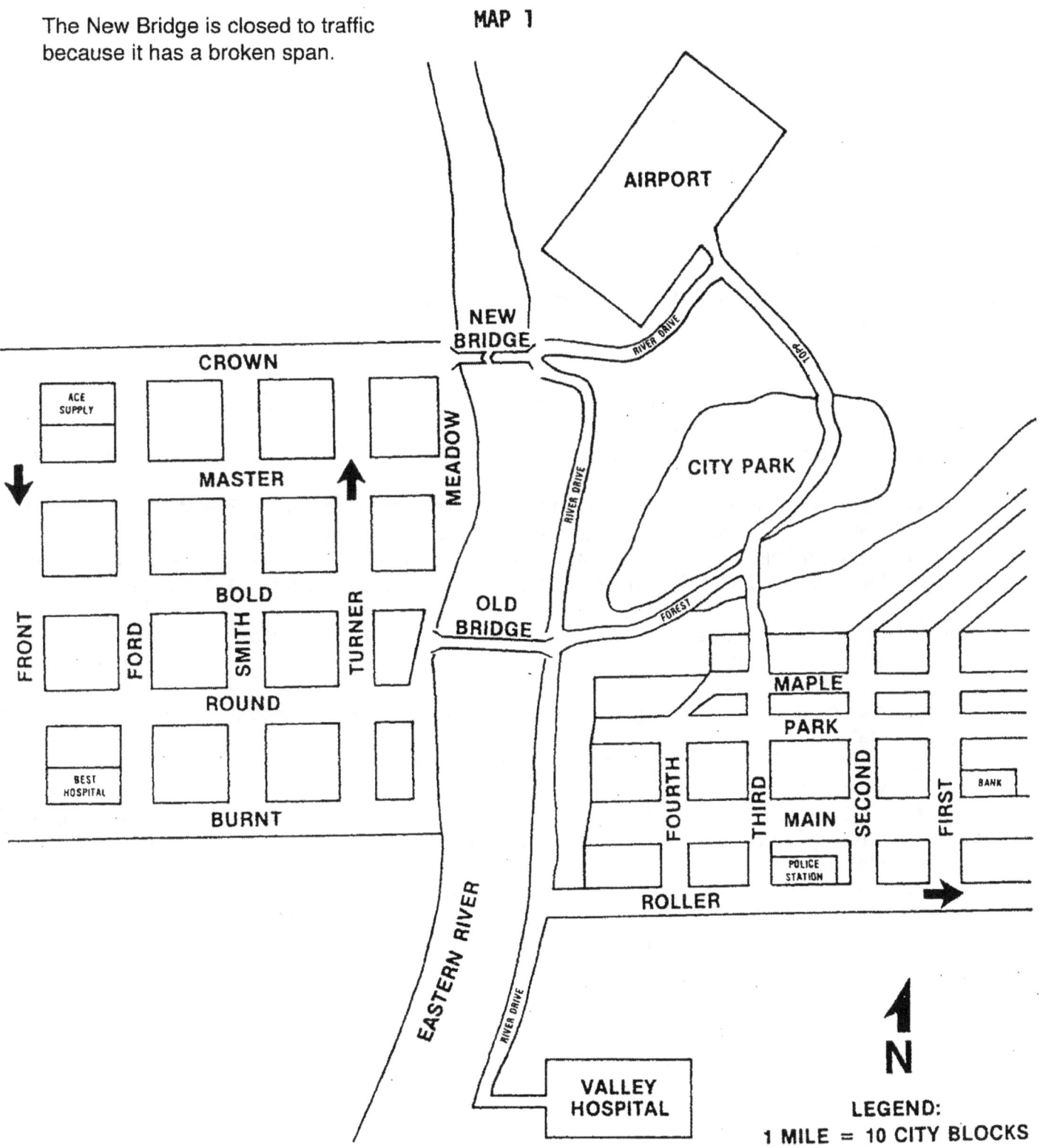

MAP 1

Arrows (→) indicate on-way traffic and direction of traffic. A street marked by an arrow is one way for the entire length of the street.

SAMPLE QUESTIONS

1. Officers in a patrol car which is at the Airport receive a call for assistance at Best Hospital. The shortest route without breaking the law is:
    A. Southwest on River Drive, right on Forest, cross Old Bridge, south on Meadow, and west on Burnt to hospital entrance.
    B. Southwest on River Drive, right on New Bridge, left on Meadow, west on Burnt to hospital entrance.
    C. Southwest on River Drive, right on Old Bridge, left on Turner, right on Burnt to hospital entrance.
    D. North on River Drive to Topp, through City Park to Forest, cross Old Bridge, left on Meadow, west on Burnt to hospital entrance.

2. After returning to the police station, the officers receive a call to pick up injured persons at an accident site (located on the east side of New Bridge) and return to Valley Hospital. The shortest route without breaking the law is:

    A. West on Roller, north on River Drive, left to accident scene at New Bridge, then north on River Drive to hospital entrance.
    B. North on Third, left on Forest, north on River Drive, left to accident scene at new Bridge, then south on River Drive to hospital entrance.
    C. East on Roller, left on First, west on Maple, north on Third, left on Forest, north on River Drive to accident scene at New Bridge, then south on River Drive to hospital entrance.
    D. North on Third, left on Forest, cross Old Bridge, north on Meadow to New Bridge, south on Meadow, east over Old Bridge, then south on River Drive to hospital entrance.

3. While at the Valley Hospital, the officers receive a call asking them to pick up materials at the Ace Supply and return them to the police station. The shortest route without breaking the law is:
    A. North on River Drive, cross New Bridge, west on Crown to Ace Supply, then south on Front, east on Burnt, north on Meadow, cross Old Bridge, east on Forest, south on Third to police station.
    B. North on River Drive, right on Roller to police station, then north on Third, left on Forest, cross Old Bridge, north on Meadow, west on Crown to Ace Supply.
    C. North on River Drive, cross Old Bridge, north on Meadow, west on Crown to Ace Supply, then east on Crown, south on Meadow, cross Old Bridge, east on Forest, south on Third to police station.
    D. North on River Drive, cross Old Bridge, south on Meadow, west on Burnt, north on Front to Ace Supply, then east on Crown, south on Meadow, cross Old Bridge, east on Forest, south on Third to police station.

KEY (CORRECT ANSWERS)

1. A
2. B
3. C

MAP READING

EXAMINATION SECTION
TEST 1

DIRECTIONS: Each question or incomplete statement is followed by several suggested answers or completions. Select the one that BEST answers the question or completes the statement. *PRINT THE LETTER OF THE CORRECT ANSWER IN THE SPACE AT THE RIGHT.*

Questions 1-3.

DIRECTIONS: Questions 1 through 3 are to be answered SOLELY on the basis of the map which appears on the next page. The flow of traffic is indicated by the arrow. If there is only one arrow shown, then traffic flows only in the direction indicated by the arrow. If there are two arrows shown, then traffic flows in both directions. You must follow the flow of traffic.

2 (#1)

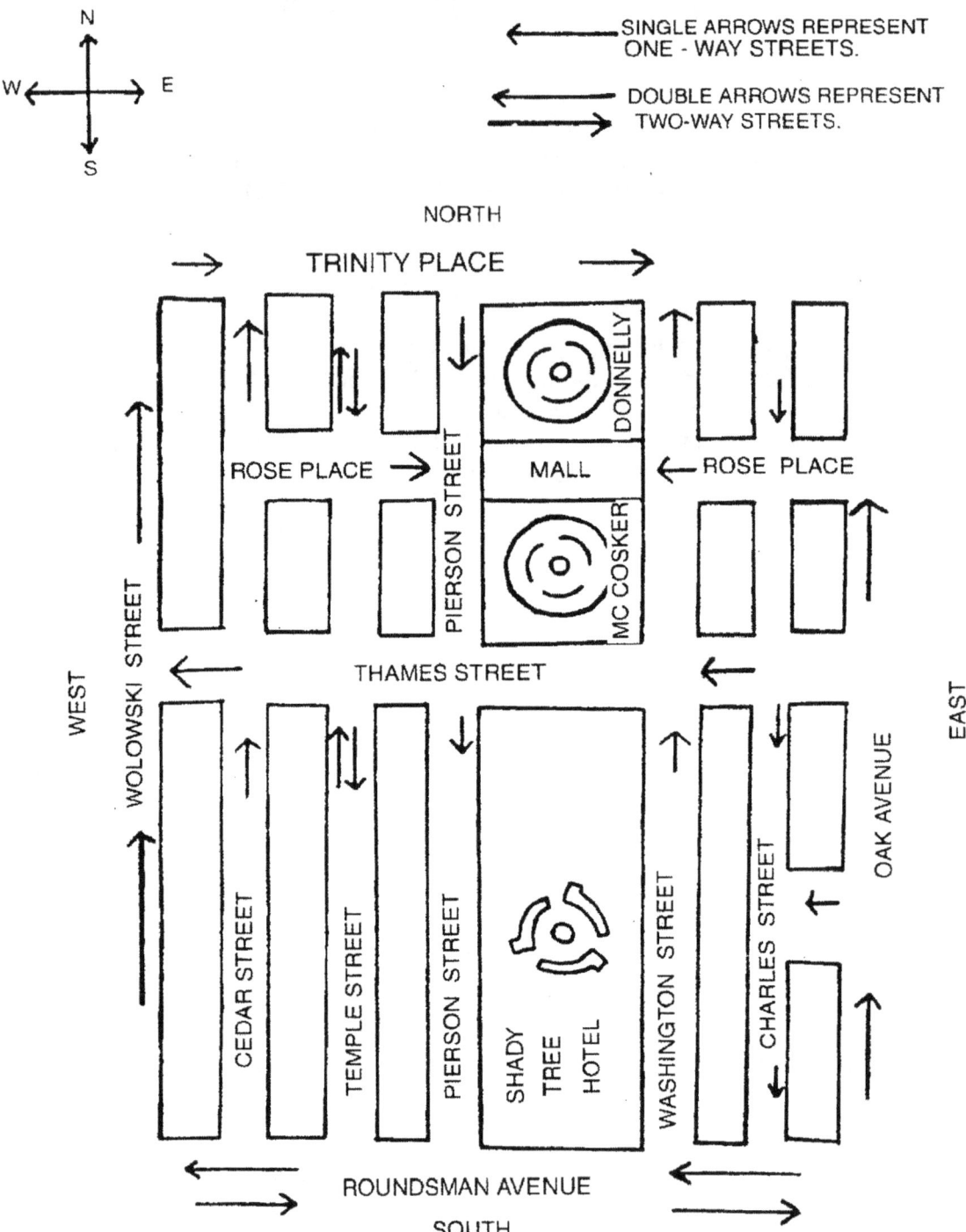

1. Police Officers Simms and O'Brien are located at Roundsman Avenue and Washington Street. The radio dispatcher has assigned them to investigate a motor vehicle accident at the corner of Pierson Street and Rose Place.
   Which one of the following is the SHORTEST route for them to take in their patrol car, making sure to obey all traffic regulations?
   Travel

   A. west on Roundsman Avenue, then north on Temple Street, then east on Thames Street, then north on Pierson Street to Rose Place
   B. east on Roundsman Avenue, then north on Oak Avenue, then west on Rose Place to Pierson Street
   C. west on Roundsman Avenue, then north on Temple Street, then east on Rose Place to Pierson Street
   D. east on Roundsman Avenue, then north on Oak Avenue, then west on Thames Street, then north on Temple Street, then east on Rose Place to Pierson Street

2. Police Officers Sears and Castro are located at Cedar Street and Roundsman Avenue. They are called to respond to the scene of a burglary at Rose Place and Charles Street. Which one of the following is the SHORTEST route for them to take in their patrol car, making sure to obey all traffic regulations?
   Travel

   A. east on Roundsman Avenue, then north on Oak Avenue, then west on Rose Place to Charles Street
   B. east on Roundsman Avenue, then north on Washington Street, then east on Rose Place to Charles Street
   C. west on Roundsman Avenue, then north on Wolowski Street, then east on Trinity Place, then south on Charles Street to Rose Place
   D. east on Roundsman Avenue, then north on Charles Street to Rose Place

3. Police Officer Glasser is in an unmarked car at the intersection of Rose Place and Temple Street when he begins to follow two robbery suspects. The suspects go south for two blocks, then turn left for two blocks, then make another left turn for one more block. The suspects realize they are being followed and make a left turn and travel two more blocks and then make a right turn.
   In what direction are the suspects now headed?

   A. North   B. South   C. East   D. West

Questions 4-6.

DIRECTIONS: Questions 4 through 6 are to be answered SOLELY on the basis of the following map. The flow of traffic is indicated by the arrows. If there is only one arrow shown, then traffic flows only in the direction indicated by the arrow. If there are two arrows shown, then traffic flows in both directions. You must follow the flow of traffic.

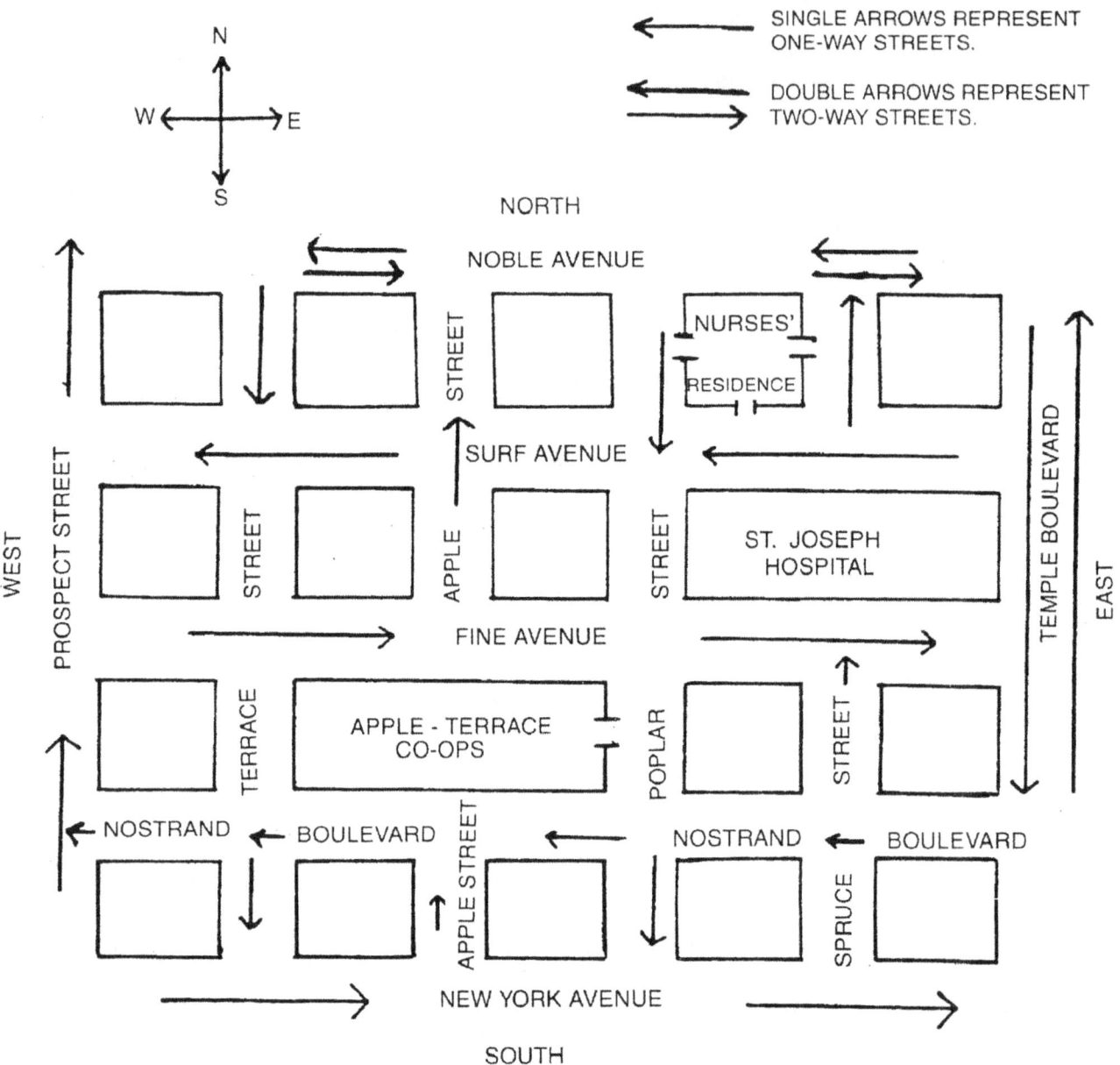

4. Police Officers Gannon and Vine are located at the intersection of Terrace Street and Surf Avenue when they receive a call from the radio dispatcher stating that they need to respond to an attempted murder at Spruce Street and Fine Avenue.
Which one of the following is the SHORTEST route for them to take in their patrol car, making sure to obey all traffic regulations?
Travel _____ to Spruce Street.

    A. west on Surf Avenue, then north on Prospect Street, then east on Noble Avenue, then south on Poplar Street, then east on Fine Avenue
    B. east on Surf Avenue, then south on Poplar Street, then east on Fine Avenue
    C. west on Surf Avenue, then south on Prospect Street, then east on Fine Avenue
    D. south on Terrace Street, then east on Fine Avenue

5. Police Officers Sears and Ronald are at Nostrand Boulevard and Prospect Street. They receive a call assigning them to investigate a disruptive group of youths at Temple Boulevard and Surf Avenue.
   Which one of the following is the SHORTEST route for them to take in their patrol car, making sure to obey all traffic regulations?
   Travel

   A. north on Prospect Street, then east on Surf Avenue to Temple Boulevard
   B. north on Prospect Street, then east on Noble Avenue, then south on Temple Boulevard to Surf Avenue
   C. north on Prospect Street, then east on Fine Avenue, then north on Temple Boulevard to Surf Avenue
   D. south on Prospect Street, then east on New York Avenue, then north on Temple Boulevard to Surf Avenue

6. While on patrol at Prospect Street and New York Avenue, Police Officers Ross and Rock are called to a burglary in progress near the entrance to the Apple-Terrace Co-ops on Poplar Street midway between Fine Avenue and Nostrand Boulevard.
   Which one of the following is the SHORTEST route for them to take in their patrol car, making sure to obey all traffic regulations?
   Travel _____ Poplar Street.

   A. east on New York Avenue, then north
   B. north on Prospect Avenue, then east on Fine Avenue, then south
   C. north on Prospect Street, then east on Surf Avenue, then south
   D. east on New York Avenue, then north on Temple Boulevard, then west on Surf Avenue, then south

Questions 7-8.

DIRECTIONS: Questions 7 and 8 are to be answered SOLELY on the basis of the map which appears below. The flow of traffic is indicated by the arrows. If there is only one arrow shown, then traffic flows only in the direction indicated by the arrow. If there are two arrows shown, then traffic flows in both directions. You must follow the flow of traffic.

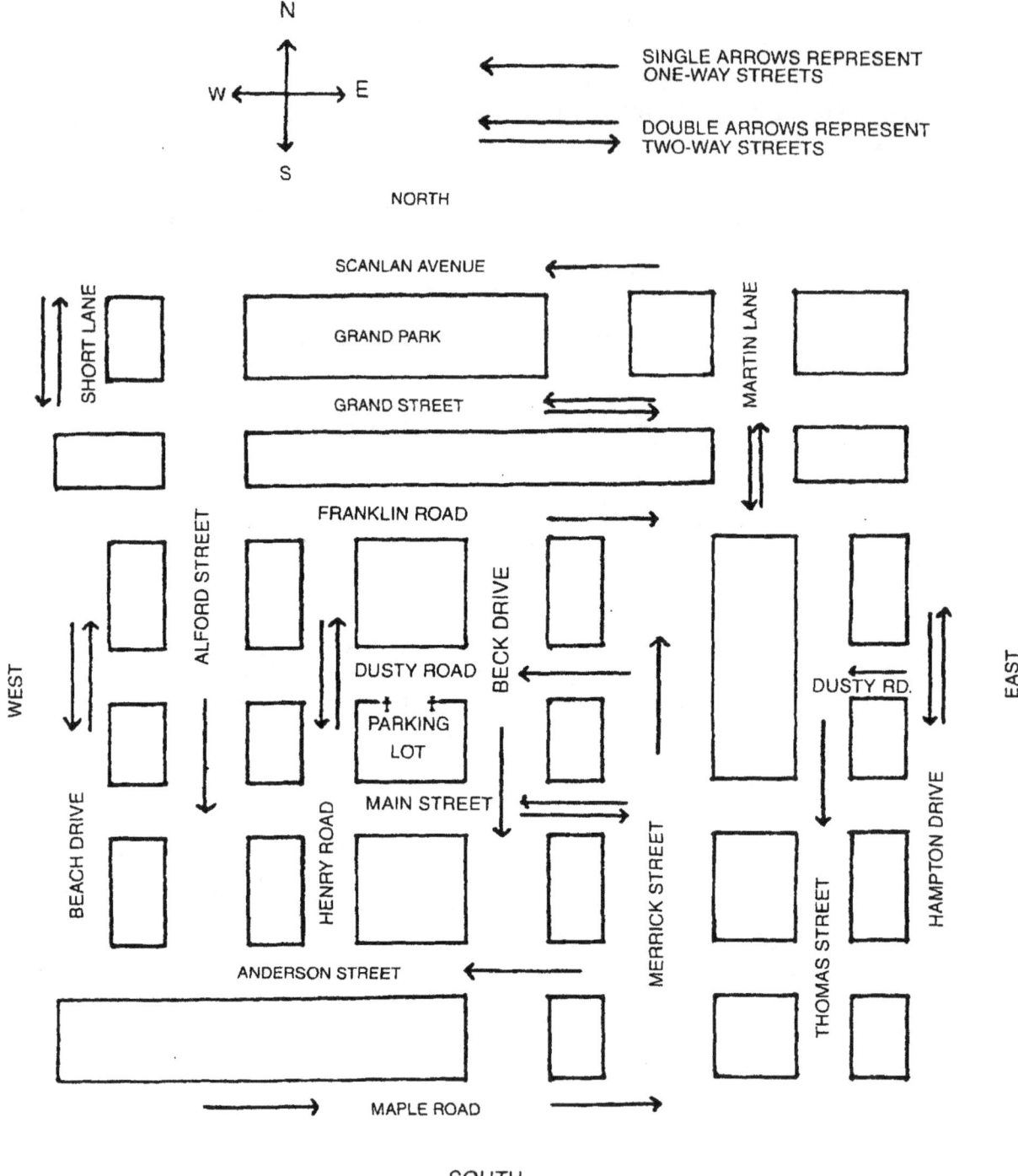

7. Police Officers Gold and Warren are at the intersection of Maple Road and Hampton Drive. The radio dispatcher has assigned them to investigate an attempted auto theft in the parking lot on Dusty Road.
Which one of the following is the SHORTEST route for the officers to take in their patrol car to get to the entrance of the parking lot on Dusty Road, making sure to obey all traffic regulations?
Travel _____ to the parking lot entrance.

7. ____

A. north on Hampton Drive, then west on Dusty Road
B. west on Maple Road, then north on Beck Drive, then west on Dusty Road
C. north on Hampton Drive, then west on Anderson Street, then north on Merrick Street, then west on Dusty Road
D. west on Maple Road, then north on Merrick Street, then west on Dusty Road

8. Police Officer Gladden is in a patrol car at the intersection of Beach Drive and Anderson Street when he spots a suspicious car. Police Officer Gladden calls the radio dispatcher to determine if the vehicle was stolen. Police Officer Gladden then follows the vehicle north on Beach Drive for three blocks, then turns right and proceeds for one block and makes another right. He then follows the vehicle for two blocks, and then they both make a left turn and continue driving. Police Officer Gladden now receives a call from the dispatcher stating the car was reported stolen and signals for the vehicle to pull to the side of the road.
In what direction was Police Officer Gladden heading at the time he signaled for the other car to pull over?   8._____

A. North   B. East   C. South   D. West

Questions 9-10.

DIRECTIONS: Questions 9 and 10 are to be answered SOLELY on the basis of the map which appears on the following page. The flow of traffic is indicated by the arrows. If there is only one arrow shown, then traffic flows only in the direction indicated by the arrow. If there are two arrows shown, then traffic flows in both directions. You must follow the flow of traffic.

8 (#1)

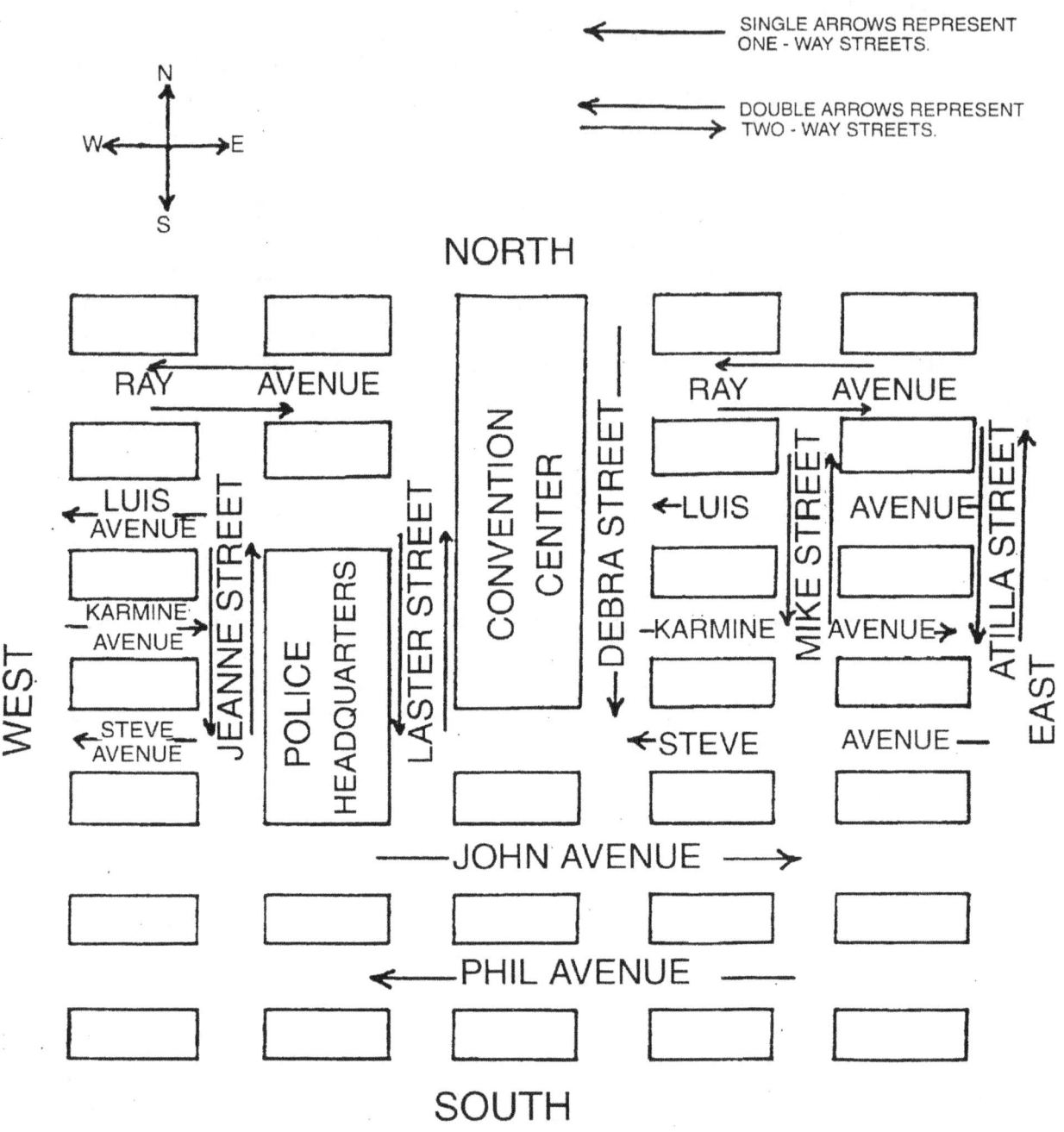

9. While in a patrol car located at Ray Avenue and Atilla Street, Police Officer Ashley receives a call from the dispatcher to respond to an assault at Jeanne Street and Karmine Avenue.
Which one of the following is the SHORTEST route for Officer Ashley to follow in his patrol car, making sure to obey all traffic regulations?
Travel

   A. south on Atilla Street, west on Luis Avenue, south on Debra Street, west on Steve Avenue, north on Lester Street, west on Luis Avenue, then one block south on Jeanne Street
   B. south on Atilla Street, then four blocks west on Phil Avenue, then north on Jeanne Street to Karmine Avenue

9. _____

C. west on Ray Avenue to Debra Street, then five blocks south to Phil Avenue, then west to Jeanne Street, then three blocks north to Karmine Avenue
D. south on Atilla Street, then four blocks west on John Avenue, then north on Jeanne Street to Karmine Avenue

10. After taking a complaint report from the assault victim, Officer Ashley receives a call from the dispatcher to respond to an auto larceny in progress at the corner of Debra Street and Luis Avenue.
Which one of the following is the SHORTEST route for Officer Ashley to follow in his patrol car, making sure to obey all traffic regulations?
Travel

    A. south on Jeanne Street to John Avenue, then east three blocks on John Avenue, then north on Mike Street to Luis Avenue, then west to Debra Street
    B. south on Jeanne Street to John Avenue, then east two blocks on John Avenue, then north on Debra Street to Luis Avenue
    C. north on Jeanne Street two blocks, then east on Ray Avenue for one block, then south on Lester Street to Steve Avenue, then one block east on Steve Avenue, then north on Debra Street to Luis Avenue
    D. south on Jeanne Street to John Avenue, then east on John Avenue to Atilla Street, then north three blocks to Luis Avenue, then west to Debra Street

Questions 11-13.

DIRECTIONS: Questions 11 through 13 are to be answered SOLELY on the basis of the following map. The flow of traffic is indicated by the arrows. You must follow the flow of traffic.

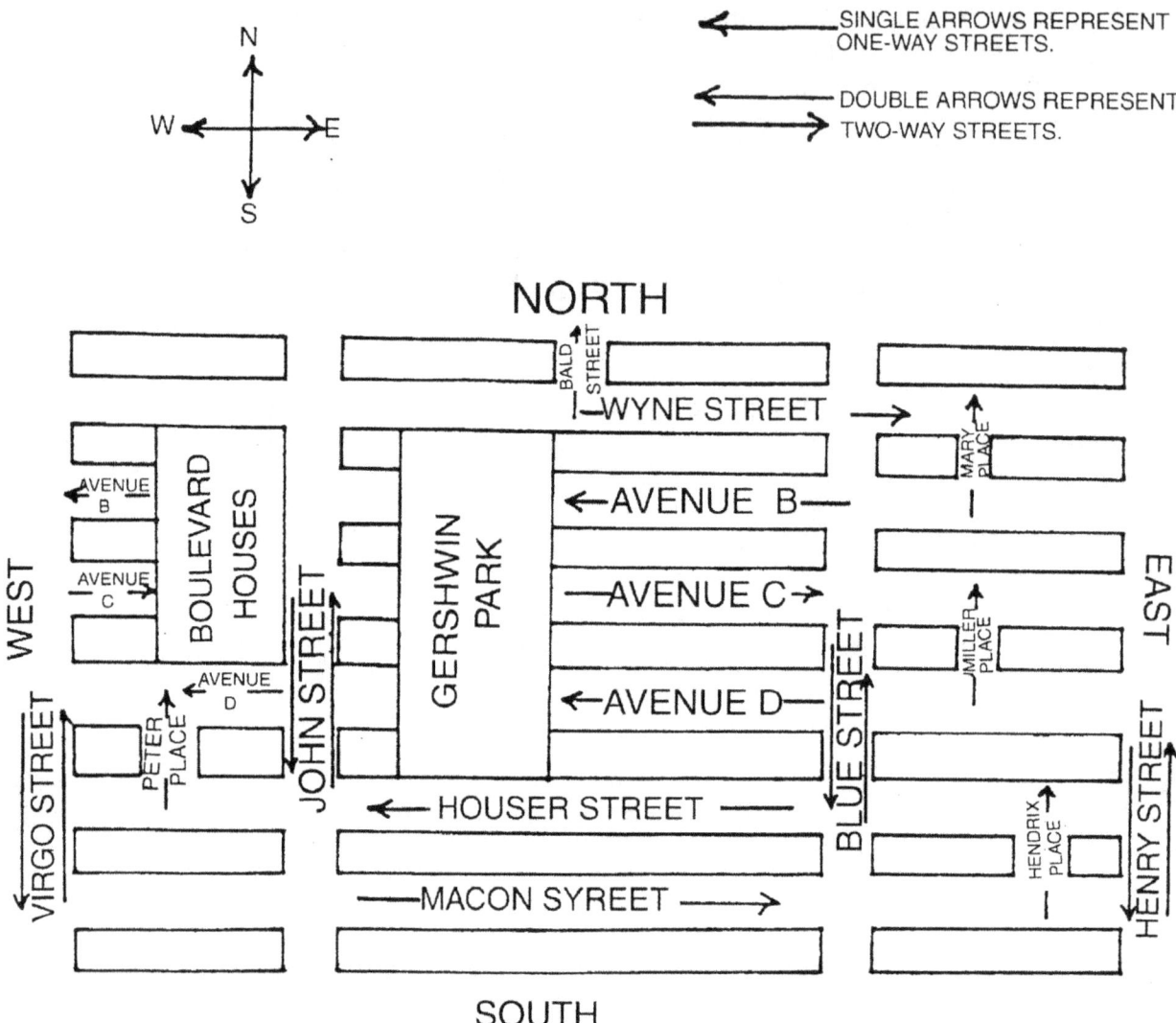

11. Police Officers Ranking and Fish are located at Wyne Street and John Street. The radio dispatcher has assigned them to investigate a motor vehicle accident at the corner of Henry Street and Houser Street.
Which one of the following is the SHORTEST route for them to take in their patrol car, making sure to obey all traffic regulations?
Travel

  A. four blocks south on John Street, then three blocks east on Houser Street to Henry Street
  B. two blocks east on Wyne Street, then two blocks south on Blue Street, then two blocks east on Avenue C, then two blocks south on Henry Street
  C. two blocks east on Wyne Street, then five blocks south on Blue Street, then two blocks east on Macon Street, then one block north on Henry Street
  D. five blocks south on John Street, then three blocks east on Macon Street, then one block north to Houser Street

12. Police Officers Rizzo and Latimer are located at Avenue B and Virgo Street. They respond to the scene of a robbery at Miller Place and Avenue D.
Which one of the following is the SHORTEST route for them to take in their patrol car, making sure to obey all traffic regulations?
Travel _____ to Miller Place.

- A. one block north on Virgo Street, then four blocks east on Wyne Street, then three blocks south on Henry Street, then one block west on Avenue D
- B. four blocks south on Virgo Street, then two blocks east on Macon Street, then two blocks north on Blue Street, then one block east on Avenue D
- C. three blocks south on Virgo Street, then east on Houser Street to Henry Street, then one block north on Henry Street, then one block west on Avenue D
- D. four blocks south on Virgo Street, then four blocks east to Henry Street, then north to Avenue D, then one block west

13. Police Officer Bendix is in an unmarked patrol car at the intersection of John Street and Macon Street when he begins to follow a robbery suspect. The suspect goes one block east, turns left, travels for three blocks, and then turns right. He drives for two blocks and then makes a right turn. In the middle of the block, the suspect realizes he is being followed and makes a u-turn. In what direction is the suspect now headed?

- A. North
- B. South
- C. East
- D. West

Questions 14-15.

DIRECTIONS: Questions 14 and 15 are to be answered SOLELY on the basis of the following map. The flow of traffic is indicated by the arrows. If there is only one arrow shown, then traffic flows only in the direction indicated by the arrow. If there are two arrows shown, then traffic flows in both directions. You must follow the flow of traffic.

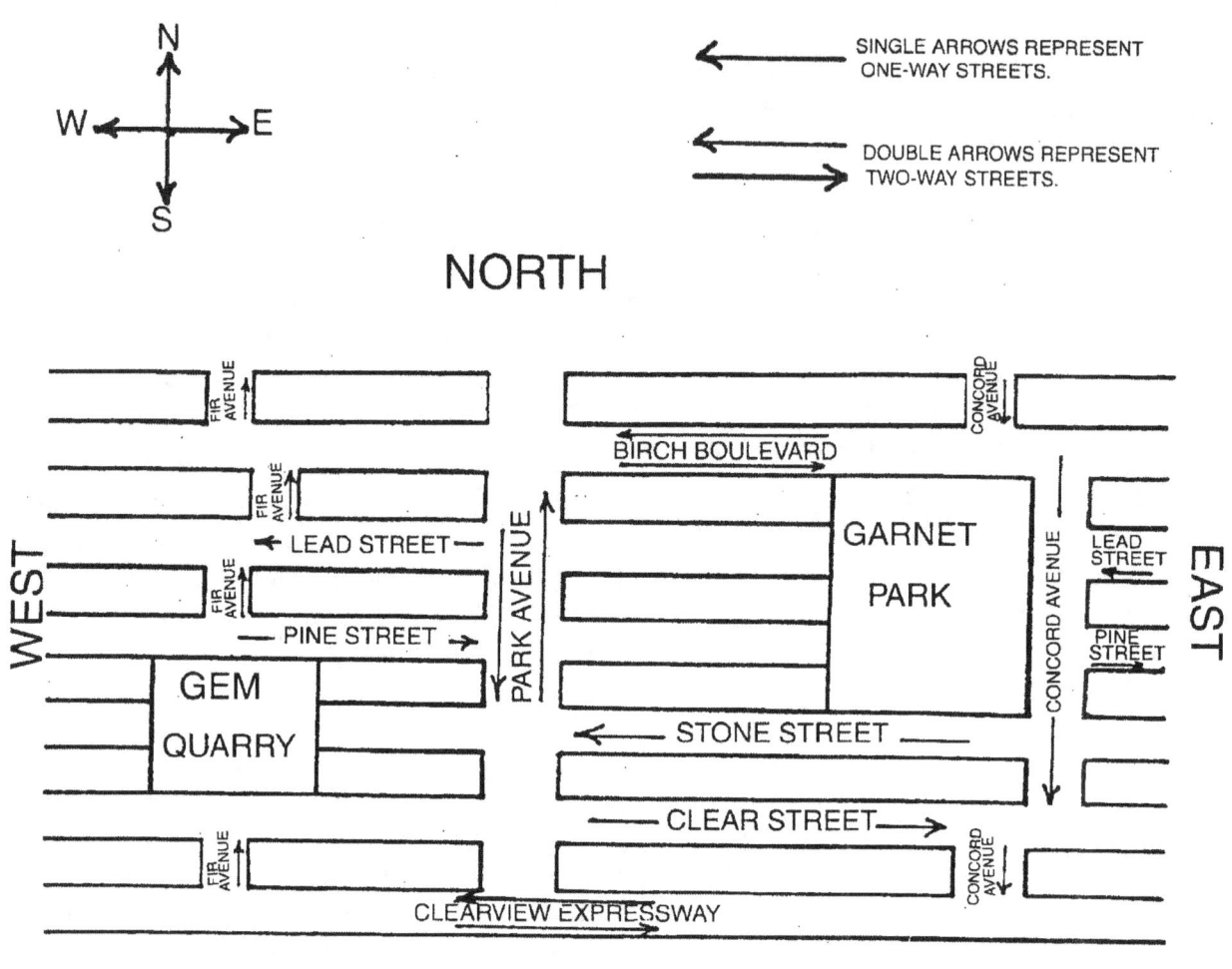

14. You are located at Fir Avenue and Birch Boulevard and receive a request to respond to a disturbance at Fir Avenue and Clear Street.
Which one of the following is the MOST direct route for you to take in your patrol car, making sure to obey all traffic regulations?
Travel

    A. one block east on Birch Boulevard, then four blocks south on Park Avenue, then one block east on Clear Street
    B. two blocks east on Birch Boulevard, then three blocks south on Concord Avenue, then two blocks west on Stone Street, then one block south on Park Avenue, then one block west on Clear Street
    C. one block east on Birch Boulevard, then five blocks south on Park Avenue, then one block west on the Clearview Expressway, then one block north on Fir Avenue
    D. two blocks south on Fir Avenue, then one block east on Pine Street, then three blocks south on Park Avenue, then one block east on the Clearview Expressway, then one block north on Fir Avenue

14.____

15. You are located at the Clearview Expressway and Concord Avenue and receive a call to respond to a crime in progress at Concord Avenue and Pine Street. Which one of the following is the MOST direct route for you to take in your patrol car, making sure to obey all traffic regulations?
Travel

 A. two blocks west on the Clearview Expressway, then one block north on Fir Avenue, then one block east on Clear Street, then four blocks north on Park Avenue, then one block east on Birch Boulevard, then two blocks south on Concord Avenue
 B. one block north on Concord Avenue, then one block west on Clear Street, then one block north on Park Avenue, then one block east on Stone Street, then one block north on Concord Avenue
 C. one block west on the Clearview Expressway, then four blocks north on Park Avenue, then one block west on Lead Street, then one block south on Fir Avenue
 D. one block west on the Clearview Expressway, then five blocks north on Park Avenue, then one block east on Birch Boulevard, then two blocks south on Concord Avenue

15.____

Questions 16-20.

DIRECTIONS: Questions 16 through 20 are to be answered SOLELY on the basis of the following map. The flow of traffic is indicated by the arrows. You must follow the flow of traffic.

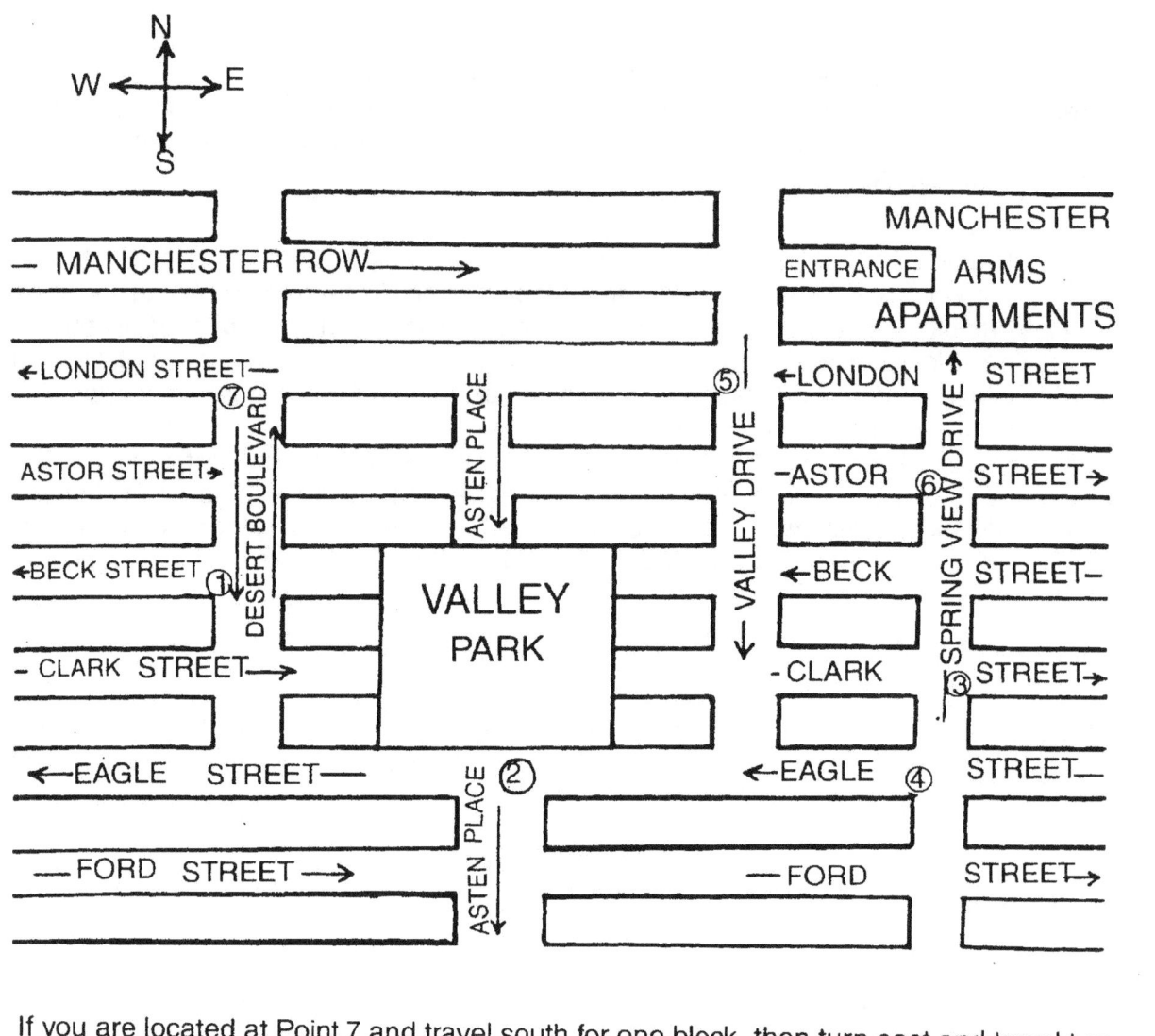

16. If you are located at Point 7 and travel south for one block, then turn east and travel two blocks, then turn south and travel two blocks, then turn east and travel one block, you will be CLOSEST to Point

    A. 2   B. 3   C. 4   D. 6

17. If you are located at Point 3 and travel north for one block, and then turn west and travel one block, and then turn south and travel two blocks, and then turn west and travel one block, you will be CLOSEST to Point

    A. 1   B. 2   C. 4   D. 6

18. You are located at Astor Street and Spring View Drive. You receive a call of a crime in progress at the intersection of Beck Street and Desert Boulevard.
    Which one of the following is the MOST direct route for you to take in your patrol car, making sure to obey all traffic regulations?
    Travel

    A. one block north on Spring View Drive, then three blocks west on London Street, then two blocks south on Desert Boulevard
    B. three blocks west on Astor Street, then one block south on Desert Boulevard

C. one block south on Spring View Drive, then three blocks west on Beck Street
D. three blocks south on Spring View Drive, then three blocks west on Eagle Street, then two blocks north on Desert Boulevard

19. You are located on Clark Street and Desert Boulevard and must respond to a disturbance at Clark Street and Spring View Drive.
Which one of the following is the MOST direct route for you to take in your patrol car, making sure to obey all traffic regulations?
Travel

   A. two blocks north on Desert Boulevard, then three blocks east on Astor Street, then two blocks south on Spring View Drive
   B. one block south on Desert Boulevard, then three blocks east on Eagle Street, then one block north on Spring View Drive
   C. two blocks north on Desert Boulevard, then two blocks east on Astor Street, then three blocks south on Valley Drive, then one block east on Eagle Street, then one block north on Spring View Drive
   D. two blocks north on Desert Boulevard, then two blocks east on Astor Street, then two blocks south on Valley Drive, then one block east on Clark Street

20. You are located at Valley Drive and Beck Street and receive a call to respond to the corner of Asten Place and Astor Street.
Which one of the following is the MOST direct route for you to take in your patrol car, making sure to obey all traffic regulations?
Travel _____ on Astor Street.

   A. one block north on Valley Drive, then one block west
   B. two blocks south on Valley Drive, then one block east on Eagle Street, then three blocks north on Spring View Drive, then two blocks west
   C. two blocks south on Valley Drive, then two blocks west on Eagle Street, then three blocks north on Desert Boulevard, then one block east
   D. one block south on Valley Drive, then one block east on Clark Street, then two blocks north on Spring View Drive, then two blocks west

KEY (CORRECT ANSWERS)

1.	C	11.	B
2.	A	12.	A
3.	A	13.	A
4.	D	14.	C
5.	C	15.	D
6.	B	16.	B
7.	C	17.	B
8.	B	18.	A
9.	A	19.	D
10.	A	20.	C

EXAMINATION SECTION
TEST 1

DIRECTIONS: Each question or incomplete statement is followed by several suggested answers or completions. Select the one that BEST answers the question or completes the statement. *PRINT THE LETTER OF THE CORRECT ANSWER IN THE SPACE AT THE RIGHT.*

Questions 1-9.

DIRECTIONS: Questions 1 through 9 measure your ability to (1) determine whether statements from witnesses say essentially the same thing, and (2) determine the evidence need to make it reasonably certain that a particular conclusion is true.

1. Which of the following pairs of statements say essentially the same thing in two different ways?
   I. The only time the machine's red light is on is when the door is locked.
      If the machine's door is locked, the red light is on.
   II. Some gray-jacketed cables are connected to the blower.
      If a cable is connected to the blower, it must be gray-jacketed.
   The CORRECT answer is:
   A. I only   B. I and II   C. II only   D. Neither I nor II

   1.____

2. Which of the following pairs of statements say essentially the same thing in two different ways?
   I. If you live on Maple Street, your child is in the Valley District.
      If your child is in the Valley District, you must live on Maple Street.
   II. All the Smith children are brown-eyed.
      If a child is brown-eyed, it is not one of the Smith children.
   The CORRECT answer is:
   A. I only   B. I and II   C. II only   D. Neither I nor II

   2.____

3. Which of the following pairs of statements say essentially the same thing in two different ways?
   I. If it's Monday, Mrs. James will be here.
      Mrs. James is here every Monday.
   II. Most people in the Drama Club do not have stage fright, but everyone in the Drama Club wants to be noticed.
      Some people in the Drama Club have stage fright and want to be noticed.
   The CORRECT answer is:
   A. I only   B. I and II   C. II only   D. Neither I nor II

   3.____

4. Which of the following pairs of statements say essentially the same thing in two different ways?
   I. If you are older than 65, you will get a senior's discount.
      Either you will get a senior's discount, or you are not older than 65.
   II. Every cadet in Officer Johnson's class has passed the firearms safety course.
       No cadet that has failed the firearms safety course is in Officer Johnson's class.
   The CORRECT answer is:
   A. I only   B. I and II   C. II only   D. Neither I nor II

5. Summary of Evidence Collected to Date:
   Most people in the Greenlawn housing project do not have criminal records.
   Prematurely Drawn Conclusion:
   Some people in Greenlawn who have been crime victims have criminal records themselves.
   Which of the following pieces of evidence, if any, would make it *reasonably certain* that the conclusion drawn is TRUE?
   A. Some of those who live in the Greenlawn project have been arrested or convicted of "victimless" crimes.
   B. Most people in Greenlawn have been the victims of crime.
   C. Everyone in Greenlawn has been the victim of crime.
   D. None of the above

6. Summary of Evidence Collected to Date:
   Every drug dealer in the Oak Lawn neighborhood wears blue and carries a Glock.
   Prematurely Drawn Conclusion:
   A person in the Oak Lawn neighborhood who carries a Glock is a drug dealer.
   Which of the following pieces of evidence, if any, would make it *reasonably certain* that the conclusion drawn is TRUE?
   A. In the Oak Lawn neighborhood, only drug dealers wear blue.
   B. Drug dealers in Oak Lawn only carry Glocks when they're dealing drugs.
   C. In the Oak Lawn neighborhood, only drug dealers carry Glocks.
   D. None of the above

7. Summary of Evidence Collected to Date:
   I. Dr. Jones is older than Dr. Gupta.
   II. Dr. Gupta and Dr. Unruh were born on the same day.
   Prematurely Drawn Conclusion:
   Dr. Gupta does not work in the emergency room.
   Which of the following pieces of evidence, if any, would make it *reasonably certain* that the conclusion drawn is TRUE?
   A. Dr. Jones is older than Dr. Unruh.
   B. Dr. Jones works in the emergency room.
   C. Every doctor in the emergency room is older than Dr. Unruh.
   D. None of the above

8. Summary of Evidence Collected to Date:
   I. On the street, a "dose" of a certain drug contains four "drams."
   II. A person can trade three "rolls" of a drug for a "plunk."
   Prematurely Drawn Conclusion:
   A plunk is the most valuable amount of the drug on the street.
   Which of the following pieces of evidence, if any, would make it *reasonably certain* that the conclusion drawn is TRUE?
   A. A person can trade five doses for two rolls.
   B. A dram contains two rolls.
   C. A roll is larger than a dram.
   D. None of the above

9. Summary of Evidence Collected to Date:
   Sam is a good writer and editor.
   Prematurely Drawn Conclusion:
   Sam is qualified for the job.
   Which of the following pieces of evidence, if any, would make it *reasonably certain* that the conclusion drawn is TRUE?
   A. The job calls for good writing and editing skills.
   B. A person who is not a good editor could still apply for the job on the strength of his/her writing skills.
   C. If Sam applies for the job, he must be both a good writer and editor.
   D. None of the above

Questions 10-14.

DIRECTIONS: Questions 10 through 14 refer to Map #7 and measure your ability to orient yourself within a given section of town, neighborhood or particular area. Each of the questions describes a starting point and a destination. Assume that you are driving a car in the area shown on the map accompanying the questions. Use the map as a basis for the shortest way to get from one point to another without breaking the law.
On the map, a street marked by arrows, or by arrows and the words "One Way," indicates one-way travel, and should be assumed to be one-way for the entire length, even when there are breaks or jogs in the street. EXCEPTION: A street that does not have the same name over the full length.

Map #7.

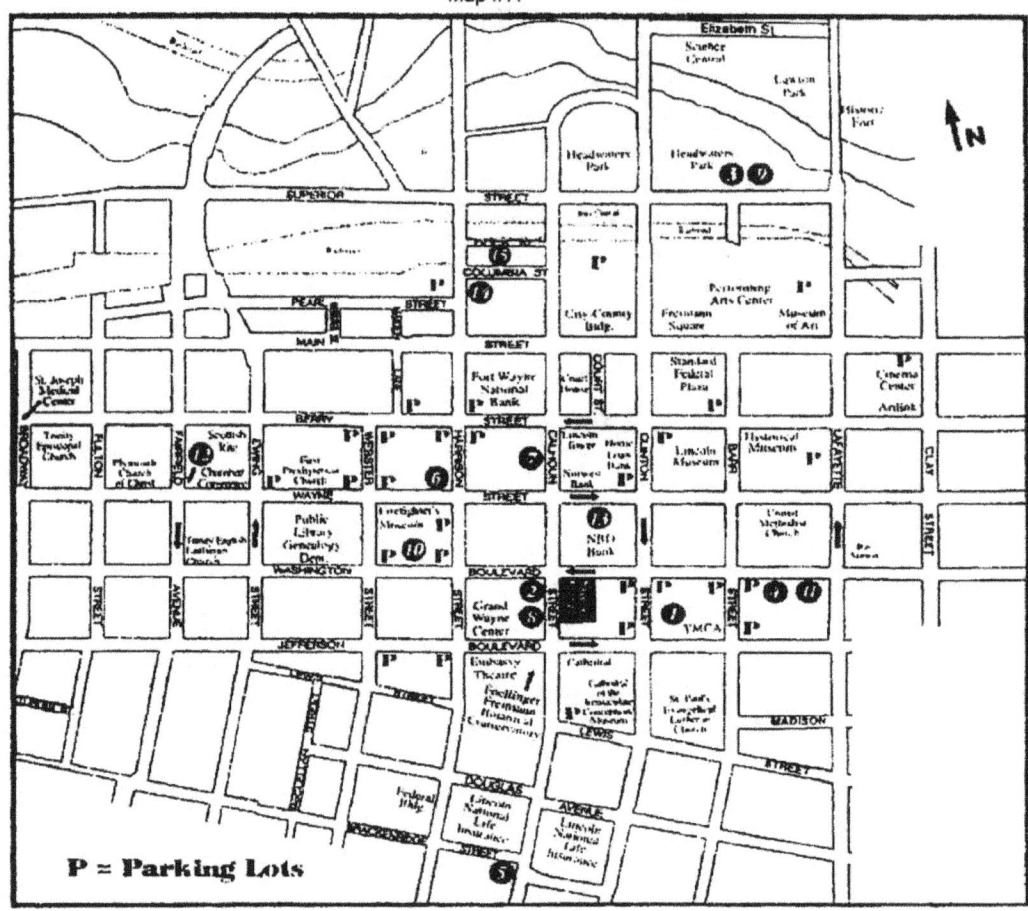

10. The SHORTEST legal way from Trinity Episcopal Church to Science Central is   10.____
    A. east on Berry, north on Clinton, east on Elizabeth
    B. east on Berry, north on Lafayette, west on Elizabeth
    C. north on Fulton, east on Main, north on Lafayette, west on Elizabeth
    D. north on Fulton, east on Main, north on Calhoun

11. The SHORTEST legal way from the Grand Wayne Center to the Museum of   11.____
    Art is
    A. north on Harrison, east on Superior, south on Lafayette
    B. east on Washington Blvd., north on Lafayette
    C. east on Jefferson Blvd., north on Clinton, east on Main
    D. east on Jefferson Blvd., north on Lafayette

12. The SHORTEST legal way from the Embassy Theatre too the City/County   12.____
    Building is
    A. west on Jefferson Blvd., north on Ewing, east on Main
    B. east on Jefferson Blvd., north on Lafayette, west on Main
    C. east on Jefferson Blvd., north on Clinton
    D. north on Harrison, east on Main

13. The SHORTEST legal way from the YMCA to the Firefighter's Museum is 13.____
    A. west on Jefferson Blvd., north on Webster
    B. north on Barr, west on Washington Blvd., north on Webster
    C. north on Barr, west on Wayne
    D. north on Barr, west on Berry, south on Webster

14. The SHORTEST legal way from the Historic Fort to Freimann Square is 14.____
    A. north on Lafayette, west on Elizabeth, south on Clinton
    B. north on Lafayette, west on Elizabeth, west/south on Calhoun, east on Main
    C. south on Lafayette, west on Main
    D. south on Lafayette, west on Superior, south on Clinton

Questions 15-19.

DIRECTIONS: Questions 15 through 19 refer to Figure #7, on the following page, and measure your ability to understand written descriptions of events. Each question presents a description of an accident or event and asks you which of the five drawings in Figure #7 BEST represents it.

In the drawings, the following symbols are used:

Moving Vehicle: ⌂   Non-moving Vehicle: ▮

Pedestrian or Bicyclist: ●

The path and direction of travel of a vehicle or pedestrian is indicated by a solid line.

The path and direction of travel of each vehicle or pedestrian directly involved in a collision from the point of impact is indicated by a dotted line.

In the space at the right, print the letter of the drawing that BEST fits the descriptions written below:

15. A driver headed northeast on Cary strikes a car in the intersection and is 15.____
    diverted north, where he collides with the rear of a car that is traveling north on Park. The northbound car is knocked into the rear of another car that is traveling north ahead of it.

16. A driver headed northeast on Cary strikes a car in the intersection and is 16.____
    diverted north, where he collides head-on with a car stopped at a traffic light in the southbound lane on Park.

17. A driver headed northeast on Cary strikes a car in the intersection and is 17.____
    diverted east, where he collides head-on with a car stopped at a traffic light in the westbound lane on Roble.

18. A driver headed east on Roble collides with the left front of a car that is turning right from Knox onto Roble. The driver swerves right after the collision and collides head-on with another car headed north on Park. 18.____

19. A driver headed northeast on Cary strikes a car in the intersection and is diverted north, where he collides with the rear of a car parked on the northbound lane on Park. 19.____

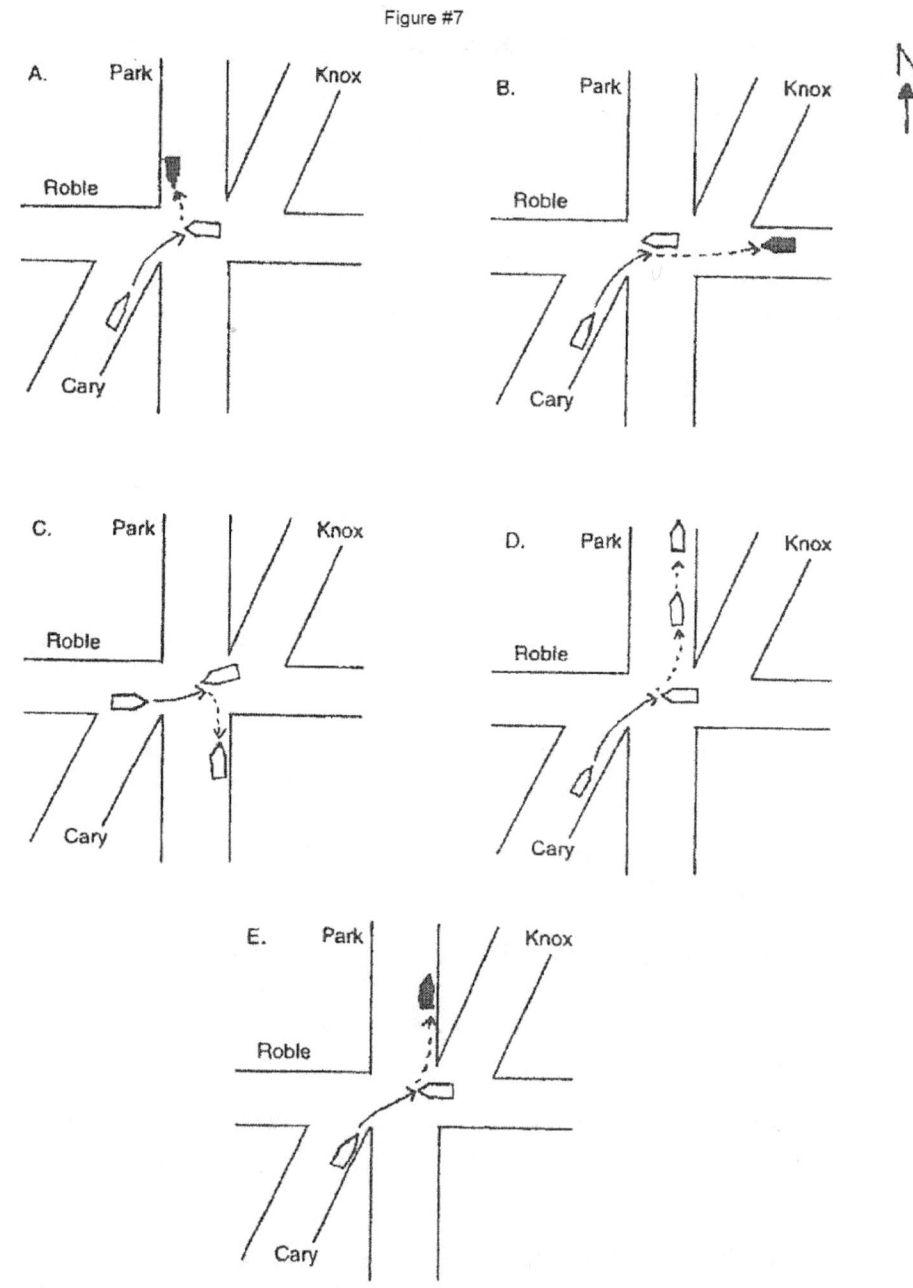

Figure #7

Questions 20-22.

DIRECTIONS: In Questions 20 through 22, choose the word or phrase CLOSEST in meaning to the word or phrase printed in capital letters.

20. JURISDICTION 20.____
 A. authority B. decision C. judgment D. argument

21. PROXY 21.____
 A. neighbor B. agent C. enforcer D. impostor

22. LARCENY 22.____
 A. theft B. assault C. deceit D. gentleness

Questions 23-25.

DIRECTIONS: Questions 22 through 25 measure your ability to do fieldwork-related arithmetic. Each question presents a separate arithmetic problem for you to solve.

23. Mr. Long has 14 employees. He has four more male employees than female employees. 23.____
 How many female employees does he have?
 A. 4 B. 5 C. 9 D. 10

24. A box of latex gloves costs $18. A crate has 12 boxes, each of which contains 48 gloves. 24.____
 How much does a crate of latex gloves cost?
 A. $216 B. $328 C. $576 D. $864

25. In a single week, the Department of Parking collected 540 quarter, 623 dimes, and 146 nickels from its parking meters. 25.____
 What was the TOTAL revenue collected from the meters during the week?
 A. $135.00 B. $154.00 C. $204.60 D. $270.30

KEY (CORRECT ANSWERS)

1. A
2. D
3. B
4. B
5. C

6. C
7. C
8. A
9. A
10. C

11. D
12. D
13. B
14. A
15. D

16. A
17. B
18. C
19. E
20. A

21. B
22. A
23. B
24. A
25. C

SOLUTIONS (QUESTIONS 1-9)

P implies Q = original statement

Not Q implies not P = contrapositive of the original statement. A statement and its contrapositive are logically equivalent.

Q implies P = converse of the original statement.

Not P implies not Q = inverse of the original statement. The converse and inverse of an original statement are logically equivalent.

P implies Q = Not P or Q

1. CORRECT ANSWER: A
   For Item I, the equivalent of the first statement would be "If the red light is on, the door is locked." This is the converse of the second statement, so it is not equivalent to the first statement. For Item II, the first statement does not guarantee that all cables that are connected to the blower must be gray-jacketed. There may very well be other cables that are connected to the blower that are not gray-jacketed. Equally possible, some gray-jacketed cables are not necessarily connected to the blower.

2. CORRECT ANSWER: D
   For Item I, the second statement is the converse of the first statement, so it is not logically equivalent. For Item II, the equivalent of the first statement is "If a child is not brown-eyed, then it is not one of the Smith children." Thus, statement II as it stands is not equivalent to statement I.

3. CORRECT ANSWER: B
   For Item I, Mrs. James is here every Monday, so we conclude that if it is Monday, she is here. (She may be here on other days as well.) For Item II, we can conclude that there are some people in the Drama Club who do have stage fright. Since everyone in the Drama Club wants to be noticed, this would include those who have stage fright.

4. CORRECT ANSWER: B
   For Item I, these two statements represent "P implies Q" and "Not P or Q," where P = Older than 65 and Q = Get a senior discount. These are equivalent statements. For Item II, these statements are contrapositive of each other and so must be equivalent. (P = Cadet in Johnson's class and Q = Passes the safety course.)

5. CORRECT ANSWER: C
   If everyone in the housing project has been a victim of crime and most of these people do not have a criminal record, we can conclude that some of them do have a criminal record. Thus, we have the situation that some of the people who live in this housing project are both a victim of crime as well as a perpetrator of crime.

6. CORRECT ANSWER: C
This choice can be written as "In this neighborhood, if a person carries a Glock, he is a drug dealer." This would lead directly to the drawn conclusion.

7. CORRECT ANSWER: C
We know that every doctor in the emergency room is older than Dr. Unruh; it is not possible for Dr. Gupta to be working in the emergency room since he is the same age as Dr. Unruh.

8. CORRECT ANSWER: A
From statement I, a dose is worth more than a dram. If 5 doses is equal to 2 rolls, then a roll is worth more than a dose. So of these three, a roll is worth the most. Finally, statement II tells us that a plunk is worth more than a roll. This means that a plunk is worth the most among all four of these categories.

9. CORRECT ANSWER: A
Sam has the qualifications of being a good writer and editor, which is exactly what is needed for the job. Therefore, Sam is qualified for this job.

TEST 2

DIRECTIONS: Each question or incomplete statement is followed by several suggested answers or completions. Select the one that BEST answers the question or completes the statement. *PRINT THE LETTER OF THE CORRECT ANSWER IN THE SPACE AT THE RIGHT.*

Questions 1-9.

DIRECTIONS: Questions 1 through 9 measure your ability to (1) determine whether statements from witnesses say essentially the same thing, and (2) determine the evidence need to make it reasonably certain that a particular conclusion is true.

To do well on this part of the test, you do NOT have to have a working knowledge of police procedures and techniques. Nor do you have to have any more familiarity with criminals and criminal behavior than that acquired from reading newspapers, listening to radio or watching TV. To do well in this part, you must read and reason carefully.

1. Which of the following pairs of statements say essentially the same thing in two different ways?
   I. If the garbage is collected today, it is definitely Wednesday.
      The garbage is collected every Wednesday.
   II. Nobody has no answer to the question.
       Everybody has at least one answer to the question.
   The CORRECT answer is:
   A. I only   B. I and II   C. II only   D. Neither I nor II

2. Which of the following pairs of statements say essentially the same thing in two different ways?
   I. If it trains, the streets will be wet.
      If the streets are wet, it has rained.
   II. All of the Duluth Five are immune from prosecution.
       No member of the Duluth Five can be prosecuted.
   The CORRECT answer is:
   A. I only   B. I and II   C. II only   D. Neither I nor II

3. Which of the following pairs of statements say essentially the same thing in two different ways?
   I. Ms. Friar will accept her promotion if and only if she is offered a 10% raise.
      For Ms. Friar to accept her promotion, it is necessary that she be offered a 10% raise.
   II. If the hydraulic lines are flushed, it is definitely inspection day.
       The hydraulic lines are flushed only on inspection days.
   The CORRECT answer is:
   A. I only   B. I and II   C. II only   D. Neither I nor II

4. Which of the following pairs of statements say essentially the same thing in two different ways?
   I. If you are tall you will get onto the basketball team.
      Unless you are tall, you will not get onto the basketball team.
   II. That raven is black.
       If that bird is black, it's a raven.
   The CORRECT answer is:
   A. I only   B. I and II   C. II only   D. Neither I nor II

5. Summary of Evidence Collected to Date:
   Every member of the Rotary Club is retired.
   Prematurely Drawn Conclusion:
   At least some people in the planning commission are retired.
   Which of the following pieces of evidence, if any, would make it *reasonably certain* that the conclusion drawn is TRUE?
   A. Retirement is a condition for membership in the Rotary Club.
   B. Every member of the planning commission has been in the Rotary Club at one time.
   C. Every member of the Rotary Club is also on the planning commission.
   D. None of the above

6. Summary of Evidence Collected to Date:
   Some of the SWAT team snipers have poor aim.
   Prematurely Drawn Conclusion:
   The snipers on the SWAT team with the worst aim also have 20/20 vision.
   Which of the following pieces of evidence, if any, would make it *reasonably certain* that the conclusion drawn is TRUE?
   A. Some of the SWAT team snipers have 20/20 vision.
   B. Every sniper on the SWAT team has 20/20 vision.
   C. Some snipers on the SWAT team wear corrective lenses.
   D. None of the above

7. Summary of Evidence Collected to Date:
   The only time Garson hears voices is on a day when he doesn't take his medication.
   Prematurely Drawn Conclusion:
   On Fridays, Garson never hears voices.
   Which of the following pieces of evidence, if any, would make it *reasonably certain* that the conclusion drawn is TRUE?
   A. Garson is supposed to take his medication every day.
   B. Garson usually undergoes shock therapy on Fridays.
   C. Garson usually takes his medication and undergoes shock therapy on Fridays.
   D. None of the above

8. Summary of Evidence Collected to Date:
   Among the three maintenance workers, Frank, Lily and Jean, Frank is not the tallest.
   Prematurely Drawn Conclusion:
   Lily is the tallest.
   Which of the following pieces of evidence, if any, would make it *reasonably certain* that the conclusion drawn is TRUE?
   A. Jean is not the tallest.
   B. Frank is the shortest.
   C. Jean is the shortest.
   D. None of the above

9. Summary of Evidence Collected to Date:
   Doctor Lyons went to the cafeteria for lunch today and did not eat dessert.
   Prematurely Drawn Conclusion:
   The cafeteria did not serve dessert.
   Which of the following pieces of evidence, if any, would make it *reasonably certain* that the conclusion drawn is TRUE?
   A. Dr. Lyons never eats dessert.
   B. When the cafeteria serves dessert, Dr. Lyons always eats it.
   C. The cafeteria rarely serves dessert when Dr. Lyons eats there.

Questions 10-14.

DIRECTIONS: Questions 10 through 14 refer to Map #8 and measure your ability to orient yourself within a given section of town, neighborhood or particular area. Each of the questions describes a starting point and a destination. Assume that you are driving a car in the area shown on the map accompanying the questions. Use the map as a basis for the shortest way to get from one point to another without breaking the law.
On the map, a street marked by arrows, or by arrows and the words "One Way," indicates one-way travel, and should be assumed to be one-way for the entire length, even when there are breaks or jogs in the street. EXCEPTION: A street that does not have the same name over the full length.

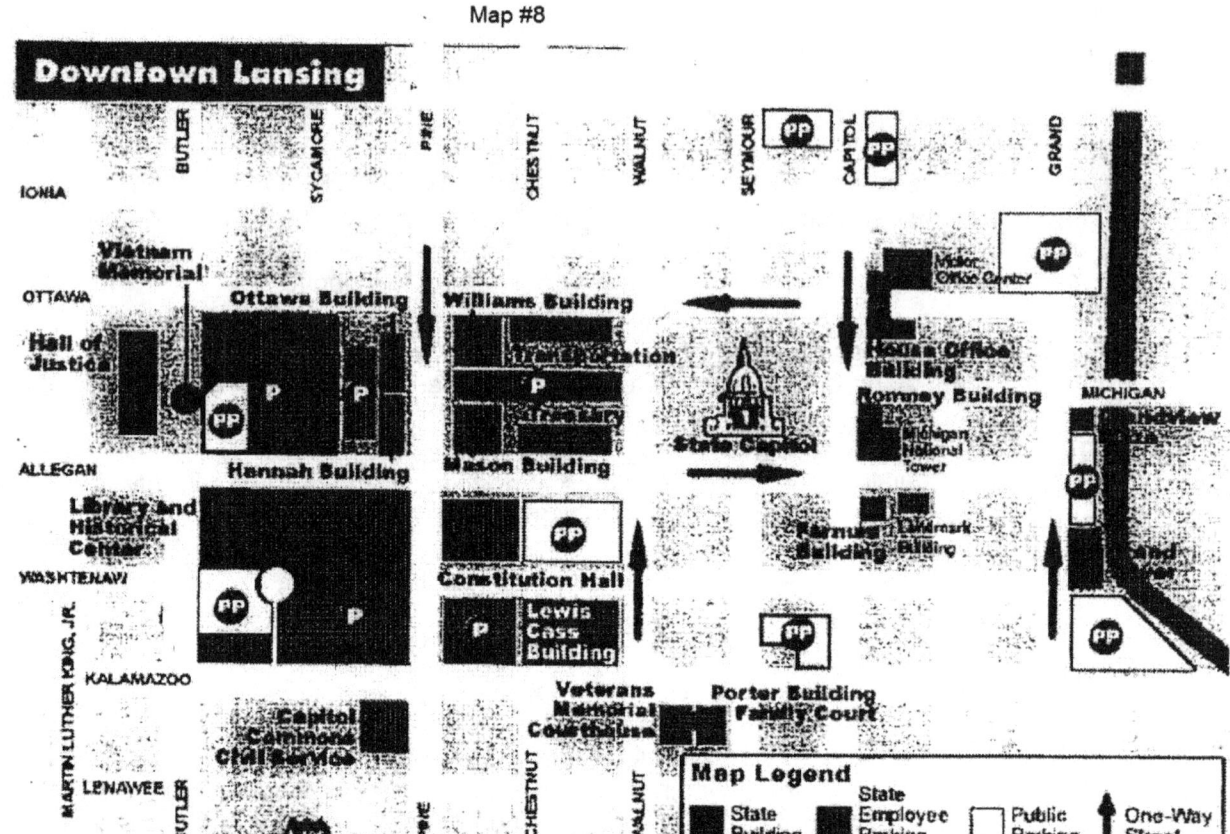

10. The SHORTEST legal way from the Library and Historical Center to Grandview Plaza is
    A. south on Butler, east on Kalamazoo, north on Grand
    B. east on Allegan, north on Grand
    C. north on Butler, east on Ionia, south on Grand
    D. north on Martin Luther King, Jr., east on Ottawa, south on Pine, east on Allegan, north on Grand

10.____

11. The SHORTEST legal way from the Victor Office Center to the Mason Building is
    A. west on Ottawa, south on Pine
    B. south on Capitol, west on Allegan, north on Pine
    C. south on Capitol, west on Washtenaw, north on Walnut, west on Allegan
    D. west on Ottawa, north on Seymour, west on Ionia, south on Pine

11.____

12. The SHORTESST legal way from the Treasury to the Hall of Justice is
    A. north on Walnut, west on Ottawa, south on Martin Luther King, Jr.
    B. west on Allegan
    C. east on Allegan, north on Grand, west on Ottawa, south on Martin Luther King. Jr.
    D. south on Walnut, west on Kalamazoo, north on Martin Luther King, Jr.

12.____

5 (#2)

13. The SHORTEST legal way from the Veterans Memorial Courthouse to the House Office Building is   13.____
    A. north on Walnut, east on Ottawa
    B. east on Kalamazoo, north on Capitol
    C. east on Kalamazoo, north on Grand, west on Ottawa
    D. north on Walnut, east on Allegan, north on Capitol

14. The SHORTEST legal way from Grand Tower to Constitution Hall is   14.____
    A. west on Washtenaw
    B. north on Grand, west on Allegan, south on Pine
    C. north on Grand, west on Ottaway, south on Pine
    D. south on Grand, west on Kalamazoo, north on Pine

Questions 15-19.

DIRECTIONS: Questions 15 through 19 refer to Figure #8, on the following page, and measure your ability to understand written descriptions of events. Each question presents a description of an accident or event and asks you which of the five drawings in Figure #8 BEST represents it.

In the drawings, the following symbols are used:

Moving Vehicle: ⌂   Non-moving Vehicle: ▮

Pedestrian or Bicyclist: ●

The path and direction of travel of a vehicle or pedestrian is indicated by a solid line.

The path and direction of travel of each vehicle or pedestrian directly involved in a collision from the point of impact is indicated by a dotted line.

In the space at the right, print the letter of the drawing that BEST fits the descriptions written below:

15. A driver headed west on Holly runs a red light and turns left. He sideswipes a car headed south in the intersection, and then flees south on Bay. The southbound car is diverted into the rear end of a car parked in the southbound lane on Bay.   15.____

16. A driver headed east on Holly runs a red light. Another driver headed south through the intersection slams on her brakes just in time to avoid a serious collision. The eastbound driver glances off the front of the southbound car and continues east, where he collides with a car parked in the eastbound lane on Holly.   16.____

17. A driver headed east on Holly runs a red light. She strikes the left front of a westbound car that is turning left from Holly onto Bay, and then veers left and strikes the rear end of a car parked in the northbound lane on Bay.   17.____

6 (#2)

18. A driver headed north on Bay strikes the right front of a car heading south in the intersection of Bay and Holly. After the collision, the driver veers left and collides with the rear end of a car parked in the westbound lane of Holly. The southbound car veers left and collides with the rear end of a car in the eastbound lane on Holly.

18.____

19. A driver headed north on Bay strikes the left front of a car heading south in the intersection of Bay and Holly. After the collision, the driver continues north and collides with the rear end of a car parked in the northbound lane. The southbound car continues south and collides with the rear end of a car in the southbound lane.

19.____

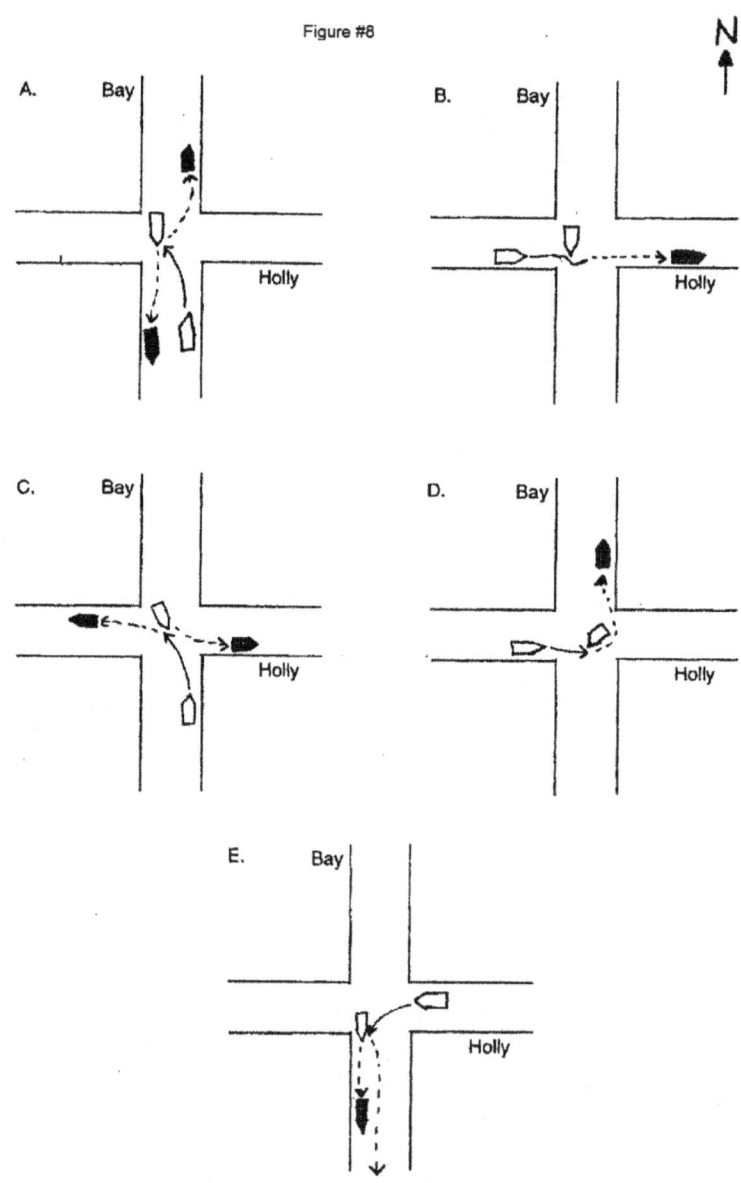

Questions 20-22.

DIRECTIONS: In Questions 20 through 22, choose the word or phrase CLOSEST in meaning to the word or phrase printed in capital letters.

20. LIABLE
    A. sensitive   B. dishonest   C. responsible   D. valid

21. CLAIM
    A. debt   B. period   C. denial   D. banishment

22. ADMISSIBLE
    A. false   B. conclusive   C. acceptable   D. indsputable

Questions 23-25.

DIRECTIONS: Questions 22 through 25 measure your ability to do fieldwork-related arithmetic. Each question presents a separate arithmetic problem for you to solve.

23. Three departments divide an $800 payment. Department 1 takes $270, and Department 2 takes $150 more than Department 3.
    How much does Department 2 take?
    A. $150   B. $190   C. $340   D. $490

24. Detective Smalley cleared 100 murder cases in five years. Each year he cleared six more than he cleared in the previous year.
    How many cases did he clear during the first year?
    A. 6   B. 8   C. 12   D. 18

25. The purchasing agent bought three binders for $2 each, four reams of copier paper for $3 each and five packs of black pens for $7 each.
    How much did the agent spend?
    A. $12.00   B. $25.20   C. $53.00   D. $72.00

KEY (CORRECT ANSWERS)

1.	B	11.	A
2.	C	12.	A
3.	B	13.	C
4.	D	14.	A
5.	C	15.	E
6.	B	16.	B
7.	D	17.	D
8.	A	18.	C
9.	B	19.	A
10.	B	20.	C

21.	A
22.	C
23.	C
24.	B
25.	C

9 (#2)

SOLUTIONS (QUESTIONS 1-9)

P implies Q = original statement

Not Q implies not P = contrapositive of the original statement. A statement and its contrapositive are logically equivalent.

Q implies P = converse of the original statement.

Not P implies not Q = inverse of the original statement. The converse and inverse of an original statement are logically equivalent.

P implies Q = Not P or Q

1. CORRECT ANSWER: B
   For Item I, we can conclude that it is Wednesday if and only if the garbage is collected.
   For Item II, the phrase "nobody has no" is equivalent to everybody has at least one."

2. CORRECT ANSWER: C
   For Item I, each statement is the converse of the other. Thus, they are not equivalent. For Item II, each statement says that each member of the Duluth Five is immune from prosecution.

3. CORRECT ANSWER: B
   For Item I, accepting a promotion is a necessary and sufficient condition for receiving a 10% raise. For Item II, we have the P implies Q condition, where P = hydraulic lines are flushed and Q = it is an inspection day.

4. CORRECT ANSWER: D
   For Item I, each statement is the converse of the other (so they are not equivalent). For Item II, the first statement simply states that a particular raven is black. The second statement says that all black birds are ravens. They are not equivalent.

5. CORRECT ANSWER: C
   The two scenarios are (a) a Rotary Club member is a subset of the set of all retirees, which is a subset of all planning commission member or (b) a Rotary Club member is a subset of all planning commission members, which is a subset of all retirees.

6. CORRECT ANSWER: B
   We know that some SWAT sniper members have poor aim. If we also know that all snipers on the SWAT team also have 20/20 vision, then we conclude that any sniper (including those with the worst aim) must have 20/20 vision.

7. CORRECT ANSWER: D
   The only way that Garson will not hear voices is if he takes his medication. The premature conclusion can only be correct if he takes his medication every Friday. None of choices A, B, or C mentions this specifically.

8. CORRECT ANSWER: A

If Frank is not the tallest and Jean is not the tallest, then the conclusion that Lily is the tallest is correct. This is a reasonable conclusion, unless all three are the same height (very unlikely).

9. CORRECT ANSWER: B

We are given that Dr. Lyons went to the cafeteria for lunch and that he did not have dessert. If Dr. Lyons always eats dessert when it is served in the cafeteria, we can conclude that the cafeteria did not serve dessert.

READING COMPREHENSION
UNDERSTANDING AND INTERPRETING WRITTEN MATERIAL
EXAMINATION SECTION
TEST 1

DIRECTIONS: Each question or incomplete statement is followed by several suggested answers or completions. Select the one that BEST answers the question or completes the statement. *PRINT THE LETTER OF THE CORRECT ANSWER IN THE SPACE AT THE RIGHT.*

Questions 1-4.

DIRECTIONS: Questions 1 through 4 are to be answered SOLELY on the basis of the information given in the paragraph below.

Abandoned cars—with tires gone, chrome stripped away, and windows smashed—have become a common sight on the city's streets. In 2000, more than 72,000 were deposited at curbs by owners who never came back, an increase of 15,000 from the year before and more than 30 times the number abandoned a decade ago. In January 2001, the city Environmental Protection Administrator asked the State Legislature to pass a law requiring a buyer of a new automobile to deposit $100 and an owner of an automobile at the time the law takes effect to deposit $50 with the State Department of Motor Vehicles. In return, they would be given a certificate of deposit which would be passed on to each succeeding owner. The final owner would get the deposit money back if he could present proof that he has disposed of his car *in an environmentally acceptable manner*. The Legislature has given no indication that it plans to rush ahead on the matter.

1. The number of cars abandoned in the city streets in 1990 was MOST NEARLY

    A. 2,500   B. 12,000   C. 27,500   D. 57,000

2. The proposed law would require a person who owned a car bought before the law was passed to deposit

    A. $100 with the State Department of Motor Vehicles
    B. $50 with the Environmental Protection Administration
    C. $100 with the State Legislature
    D. $50 with the State Department of Motor Vehicles

3. The proposed law would require the State to return the deposit money ONLY when the

    A. original owner of the car shows proof that he sold it
    B. last owner of the car shows proof that he got rid of the car in a satisfactory way
    C. owner of a car shows proof that he has transferred the certificate of deposit to the next owner
    D. last owner of a car returns the certificate of deposit

4. The MAIN idea or theme of the above article is that

   A. a proposed new law would make it necessary for car owners in the State to pay additional taxes
   B. the State Legislature is against a proposed law to require deposits from automobile owners to prevent them from abandoning their cars
   C. the city is trying to find a solution for the increasing number of cars abandoned on its streets
   D. to pay for the removal of abandoned cars the city's Environmental Protection Administrator has asked the State to fine automobile owners who abandon their vehicles

Questions 5-7.

DIRECTIONS: Questions 5 through 7 are to be answered SOLELY on the basis of the information given in the paragraph below.

The regulations applying to parking meters provide that the driver is required to deposit the appropriate coin immediately upon parking and it is illegal for him to return at a later period to extend the parking time. If there is unused time on a parking meter, another car may be parked for a period not to exceed the unused time without the deposit of a coin. Operators of commercial vehicles are not required to deposit coins while loading or unloading expeditiously. By definition, a vehicle is considered parked even though there is a driver at the wheel and the meter must be used by the driver of such car.

5. According to the above paragraph, the regulations applying to parking meters do NOT

   A. allow the driver of a parked vehicle to stay in his car
   B. consider any loading or unloading of a vehicle as parking
   C. make any distinction between an unoccupied car and one with the driver at the wheel
   D. permit a driver who has parked a car at a meter with unused parking time to put a coin in the meter

6. According to the above paragraph, it is a violation of the parking meter regulations to

   A. load and unload slowly
   B. park commercial vehicles except for loading and unloading
   C. put a second coin in the meter in order to park longer
   D. use a parking space at any time without depositing a coin

7. The above paragraph CLEARLY indicates

   A. the number of minutes a vehicle may be parked
   B. the value of the coin that is to be put in the meter
   C. what is meant by a commercial vehicle
   D. when a car may be parked free

Questions 8-13.

DIRECTIONS: Questions 8 through 13 are to be answered on the basis of the information given in the paragraph below.

There are many types of reports. One of these is the field report, which requests information specified and grouped under columns or headings. A detailed, printed form is often used in submitting field reports. However, these printed, standardized forms provide a limited amount of space. The field man is required to make the decision as to how much of the information he has should go directly into the report and how much should be left for clarification if and when he is called in to explain a reported finding. In many instances, the addition of a short explanation of the finding might relieve the reader of the report of the necessity to seek an explanation. Therefore, the basic factual information asked for by the printed report form should often be clarified by some simple explanatory statement. If this is done, the reported finding becomes meaningful to the reader of the report who is far from the scene of the subject matter dealt with in the report. The significance of that which is reported finds its expression in the adoption of certain policies, improvements, or additions essential to furthering the effectiveness of the program.

8. According to the above paragraph, the field report asks for

   A. a detailed statement of the facts
   B. field information which comes under the heading of technical data
   C. replies to well-planned questions
   D. specific information in different columns

9. According to the above paragraph, the usual printed field report form

   A. does not have much room for writing
   B. is carefully laid out
   C. is necessary for the collection of facts
   D. usually has from three to four columns

10. According to the above paragraph, the man in the field MUST decide if

    A. a report is needed at all
    B. he should be called in to explain a reported finding
    C. he should put all the information he has into the report
    D. the reader of the report is justified in seeking an explanation

11. According to the above paragraph, the man in the field may be required to

    A. be acquainted with the person or persons who will read his report
    B. explain the information he reports
    C. give advice on specific problems
    D. keep records of the amount of work he completes

12. According to the above paragraph, the value of an explanatory statement added to the factual information reported in the printed forms is that it

    A. allows the person making the report to express himself briefly
    B. forces the person making the report to think logically
    C. helps the report reader understand the facts reported
    D. makes it possible to turn in the report later

13. According to the above paragraph, the importance of the information given by the field man in his report is shown by the

    A. adoption of policies and improvements
    B. effectiveness of the field staff
    C. fact that such a report is required
    D. necessary cost studies to back up the facts

Questions 14-15.

DIRECTIONS: Questions 14 and 15 are to be answered on the basis of the information contained in the following paragraph.

The driver of the collection crew shall at all times remain in or on a department vehicle in which there is revenue. In the event such driver must leave the vehicle, he shall designate one of the other members of the crew to remain in or on the vehicle. The member of the crew so designated by the driver shall remain in or on the vehicle until relieved by the driver or another member of the crew. The vehicle may be left unattended only when there is no revenue contained therein provided, however, that in that event the vehicle shall be locked. The loss of any vehicle or any of its contents, including revenue, resulting from any deviation from this rule, shall be the responsibility of the member or members of crew who shall be guilty of such deviation.

14. The vehicle of a collection crew may be left with no one in it only if

    A. it is locked
    B. there is a crew member nearby
    C. there is no money in it
    D. there is only one member in the crew

15. If money is stolen from an unattended vehicle of a collection crew, the employee held responsible is the

    A. driver
    B. one who left the vehicle unattended
    C. one who left the vehicle unlocked
    D. one who relieved the driver

Questions 16-18.

DIRECTIONS: Questions 16 through 18 are to be answered SOLELY on the basis of the information given in the paragraph below.

Safety belts provide protection for the passengers of a vehicle by preventing them from crashing around inside if the vehicle is involved in a collision. They operate on the principle similar to that used in the packaging of fragile items. You become a part of the vehicle package, and you are kept from being tossed about inside if the vehicle is suddenly decelerated. Many injury-causing collisions at low speeds, for example at city intersections, could have been injury-free if the occupants had fastened their safety belts. There is a double advantage to the driver in that it not only protects him from harm, but prevents him from being yanked away from the wheel, thereby permitting him to maintain control of the car.

16. The principle on which seat belts work is that 16.____

    A. a car and its driver and passengers are fragile
    B. a person fastened to the car will not be thrown around when the car slows down suddenly
    C. the driver and passengers of a car that is suddenly decelerated will be thrown forward
    D. the driver and passengers of an automobile should be packaged the way fragile items are packaged

17. We can assume from the above passage that safety belts should be worn at all times because you can never tell when 17.____

    A. a car will be forced to turn off onto another road
    B. it will be necessary to shift into low gear to go up a hill
    C. you will have to speed up to pass another car
    D. a car may have to come to a sudden stop

18. Besides preventing injury, an ADDITIONAL benefit from the use of safety belts is that 18.____

    A. collisions are fewer
    B. damage to the car is kept down
    C. the car can be kept under control
    D. the number of accidents at city intersections is reduced

Questions 19-24.

DIRECTIONS: Questions 19 through 24 are to be answered on the basis of the following reading passage covering Procedures For Patrol.

PROCEDURES FOR PATROL

The primary function of all Parking Enforcement Agents assigned to patrol duty shall be to patrol assigned areas and issue summonses to violators of various sections of the City Traffic Regulations, which sections govern the parking or operation of vehicles. Parking Enforcement Agents occasionally may be called upon to distribute educational pamphlets and perform other work, at the discretion of the Bureau Chief.

Each Agent on patrol duty will be assigned a certain area (or areas) to be patrolled. These areas will be assigned during the daily roll call. Walking Cards will describe the street locations of the patrol and the manner in which the patrol is to be walked.

A Traffic Department vehicle will be provided for daily patrol assignments when necessary.

Each Agent shall accomplish an assigned field patrol in the following manner:

    a. Start each patrol at the location specified on the daily patrol sheet, and proceed as per walking instructions.
    b. Approach each metered space being utilized (each metered space in which a vehicle is parked). If the meter shows the expired flag, the member of the force shall prepare and affix a summons to the vehicle parked at meter.

c. Any vehicle in violation of any regulation governing the parking, standing, stopping, or movement of vehicles will be issued a summons.
d. No summons will be issued to a vehicle displaying an authorized vehicle identification plate of the Police Department unless the vehicle is parked in violation of the No Standing, No Stopping, Hydrant, Bus Stop, or Double Parking Regulations. Identification plates for Police Department automobiles are made of plastic and are of rectangular shape, 10 3/4" long, 3 3/4" high, black letters and numerals on a white background. The words POLICE DEPT. are printed on the face with the identification number. Identification plates for private automobiles are the same size and shape as those used on Police Department automobiles.

An Agent on patrol, when observing a person *feeding* a street meter (placing an additional coin in a meter so as to leave the vehicle parked for an additional period) shall prepare and affix a summons to the vehicle.

An Agent on patrol shall note on a computer card each missing or defective, out of order, or otherwise damaged meter.

19. Of the following, the work which the Parking Enforcement Agent performs MOST often is

    A. issuing summonses for parking violations
    B. distributing educational pamphlets
    C. assisting the Bureau Chief
    D. driving a city vehicle

20. The area to be covered by a Parking Enforcement Agent on patrol is

    A. determined by the Police Department
    B. regulated by the city Traffic Regulations
    C. marked off with red flags
    D. described on Walking Cards

21. A Parking Enforcement Agent reports a broken meter by

    A. issuing a summons
    B. making a mark on a computer card
    C. raising the flag on the broken meter
    D. attending a daily roll call

22. With respect to the use of an automobile for patrol duty,

    A. Parking Enforcement Agents must supply their own cars for patrol
    B. automobiles for patrol will be supplied by the Police Department
    C. Parking Enforcement Agents are permitted to park in a bus stop
    D. department vehicles will be provided when required for patrol

23. Parking Enforcement Agents sometimes issue summonses to drivers for *feeding* a street meter in violation of parking regulations.
    Which one of the following situations describes such a violation?
    A driver

    A. has moved from one metered space to another
    B. has parked next to a Police Department No Standing sign
    C. is parked by a meter which shows 30 minutes time still remaining
    D. has used a coin to reset the meter after his first time period expired

24. Vehicles displaying an authorized vehicle identification plate of the Police Department are allowed to park at expired meters.
Which one of the following statements describes the proper size of identification plates for private automobiles used for police work?
They

    A. are 10 3/4" long and 3 3/4" high
    B. have white letters and numerals on a black background
    C. are 3 3/4" long and 10 3/4" high
    D. have black letters and numerals on a white background

24.____

Questions 25-30.

DIRECTIONS: Questions 25 through 30 are to be answered on the basis of the following reading passage covering the Operation of Department Motor Vehicles.

OPERATION OF DEPARTMENT MOTOR VEHICLES

When operating a Traffic Department motor vehicle, a member of the force must show every courtesy to other drivers, obey all traffic signs and traffic regulations, obey all other lawful authority, and handle the vehicle in a manner which will foster safety practices in others and create a favorable impression of the Bureau, the Department, and the City. The operator and passengers MUST use the safety belts.

Driving Rules

    a. DO NOT operate a mechanically defective vehicle.
       DO NOT race engine on starting.
       DO NOT tamper with mechanical equipment.
       DO NOT run engine if there is an indication of low engine oil pressure, overheating, or no transmission oil.

    b. When parking on highway, all safety precautions must be observed.

    c. When parking in a garage or parking field, observe a maximum speed of 5 miles per hour. Place shift lever in park or neutral position, effectively apply hand brake, then shut off all ignition and light switches to prevent excess battery drain, and close all windows.

Reporting Defects

    a. Report all observed defects on Drivers' Vehicle Defect Card and on Monthly Vehicle Report Form 49 in sufficient detail so a mechanic can easily locate the source of trouble.
    b. Enter vehicle road service calls and actual time of occurrence on Monthly Vehicle Report.

Reporting Accidents

Promptly report all facts of each accident as follows: For serious accidents, including those involving personal injury, call your supervisor as soon as possible. Give all the appropriate information about the accident to your supervisor. Record vehicle registration information, including the name of the registered owner, the state, year, and serial number, and the classification marking on the license plates. Also record the operator's license number and other identifying information, and, if it applies, the injured person's age and sex. Give a full description of how the accident happened, and what happened following the accident, including the vehicles in collision, witnesses, police badge number, hospital, condition of road surface, time of day, weather conditions, location (near, far, center of intersection), and damage.

Repairs to Automobiles

When a Department motor vehicle requires repairs that cannot be made by the operator, or requires replacement of parts or accessories (including tires and tubes), or requires towing, the operator shall notify the District Commander.

When a Departmental motor vehicle is placed out of service for repairs, the Regional Commander shall assign another vehicle, if available.

Daily Operator's Report

The operator of a Department automobile shall keep a daily maintenance record of the vehicle, and note any unusual occurrences, on the Daily Operator's Report.

25. Parking Enforcement Agents who are assigned to operate Department motor vehicles on patrol are expected to

    A. disregard the posted speed limits to save time
    B. remove their seat belts on short trips
    C. show courtesy to other drivers on the road
    D. take the right of way at all intersections

26. The driver of a Department motor vehicle should

    A. leave the windows open when parking the vehicle in a garage
    B. drive the vehicle at approximately 10 miles per hour in a parking field
    C. be alert for indication of low engine oil pressure and overheated engine
    D. start a cold vehicle by racing the engine for 5 minutes

27. The reason that all defects on a Department vehicle that have been observed by its driver should be noted on a Monthly Vehicle Report Form 49 is:

    A. This action will foster better safety practices among other Agents
    B. The source of the defect may be located easily by a trained mechanic
    C. All the facts of an accident will be reported promptly
    D. The District Commander will not have to make road calls

28. If the driver of a Department vehicle is involved in an accident, an Accident Report should be made out. This Report should include a full description of how the accident happened.
    Which of the following statements would PROPERLY belong in an Accident Report?

    A. The accident occurred at the intersection of Broadway and 42nd Street.
    B. The operator of the Department motor vehicle replaced the windshield wiper.
    C. The vehicle was checked for gas and water before the patrol began.
    D. A bus passed two parked vehicles.

29. When a Department vehicle is disabled, whom should the operator notify? The

    A. Traffic Department garage
    B. Assistant Bureau Chief
    C. Police Department
    D. District Commander

30. The PROPER way for an operator of a Department vehicle to report unusual occurrences with respect to the operation of the vehicle is to

    A. follow the same procedures as for reporting a defect
    B. request the Regional Commander to assign another vehicle
    C. phone the Bureau Chief as soon as possible
    D. make a note of the circumstances on the Daily Operator's Report

KEY (CORRECT ANSWERS)

1.	A	16.	B
2.	D	17.	D
3.	B	18.	C
4.	C	19.	A
5.	C	20.	D
6.	C	21.	B
7.	D	22.	D
8.	D	23.	D
9.	A	24.	A
10.	C	25.	C
11.	B	26.	C
12.	C	27.	B
13.	A	28.	A
14.	C	29.	D
15.	B	30.	D

TEST 2

DIRECTIONS: Each question or incomplete statement is followed by several suggested answers or completions. Select the one that BEST answers the question or completes the statement. *PRINT THE LETTER OF THE CORRECT ANSWER IN THE SPACE AT THE RIGHT.*

Questions 1-4.

DIRECTIONS: Questions 1 through 4 are to be answered SOLELY on the basis of the information contained in the following passage.

Of those arrested in the city in 2003 for felonies or misdemeanors, only 32% were found guilty of any charge. Fifty-six percent of such arrestees were acquitted or had their cases dismissed. 11% failed to appear for trial, and 1% received other dispositions. Of those found guilty, only 7.4% received any sentences of over one year in jail. Only 50% of those found guilty were sentenced to any further time in jail. When considered with the low probability of arrests for most crimes, these figures make it clear that the crime control system in the city poses little threat to the average criminal. Delay compounds the problem. The average case took four appearances for disposition after arraignment. Twenty percent of all cases took eight or more appearances to reach a disposition. Forty-four percent of all cases took more than one year to disposition.

1. According to the above passage, crime statistics for 2003 indicate that

    A. there is a low probability of arrests for all crimes in the city
    B. the average criminal has much to fear from the law in the city
    C. over 10% of arrestees in the city charged with felonies or misdemeanors did not show up for trial
    D. criminals in the city are less likely to be caught than criminals in the rest of the country

2. The percentage of those arrested in 2003 who received sentences of over one year in jail amounted to MOST NEARLY

    A. .237   B. 2.4   C. 23.7   D. 24.0

3. According to the above passage, the percentage of arrestees in 2003 who were found guilty was

    A. 20% of those arrested for misdemeanors
    B. 11% of those arrested for felonies
    C. 50% of those sentenced to further time in jail
    D. 32% of those arrested for felonies or misdemeanors

4. According to the above paragraph, the number of appearances after arraignment and before disposition amounted to

    A. an average of four
    B. eight or more in 44% of the cases
    C. over four for cases which took more than a year
    D. between four and eight for most cases

Questions 5-6.

DIRECTIONS: Questions 5 and 6 are to be answered on the basis of the following paragraph.

A person who, with the intent to deprive or defraud another of the use and benefit of property or to appropriate the same to the use of the taker, or of any other person other than the true owner, wrongfully takes, obtains or withholds, by any means whatever, from the possession of the true owner or of any other person any money, personal property, thing in action, evidence of debt or contract, or article of value of any kind, steals such property and is guilty of larceny.

5. This definition from the Penal Law has NO application to the act of   5.____

    A. fraudulent conversion by a vendor of city sales tax money collected from purchasers
    B. refusing to give proper change after a purchaser has paid for an article in cash
    C. receiving property stolen from the rightful owner
    D. embezzling money from the rightful owner

6. According to the above paragraph, an auto mechanic who claimed to have a lien on an automobile for completed repairs and refused to surrender possession until the bill was paid   6.____

    A. *cannot* be charged with larceny because his repairs increased the value of the car
    B. *can* be charged with larceny because such actual possession can be construed to include intent to deprive the owner of use of the car
    C. *cannot* be charged with larceny because the withholding is temporary and such possession is not an evidence of debt
    D. *cannot* be charged with larceny because intent to defraud is lacking

Questions 7-12.

DIRECTIONS: Questions 7 through 12 are to be answered on the basis of the information given in the passage below. Assume that all questions refer to the same state described in the passage.

The courts and the police consider an *offense* as any conduct that is punishable by a fine or imprisonment. Such offenses include many kinds of acts—from behavior that is merely annoying, like throwing a noisy party that keeps everyone awake, all the way up to violent acts like murder. The law classifies offenses according to the penalties that are provided for them. In one state, minor offenses are called *violations*. A violation is punishable by a fine of not more than $250 or imprisonment of not more than 15 days, or both. The annoying behavior mentioned above is an example of a violation. More serious offenses are classified as *crimes*. Crimes are classified by the kind of penalty that is provided. A *misdemeanor* is a crime that is punishable by a fine of not more than $1,000 or by imprisonment of not more than 1 year, or both. Examples of misdemeanors include stealing something with a value of $100 or less, turning in a false alarm, or illegally possessing less than 1/8 of an ounce of a dangerous drug. A *felony* is a criminal offense punishable by imprisonment of more than 1 year. Murder is clearly a felony.

7. According to the above passage, any act that is punishable by imprisonment or by a fine is called a(n)

   A. offense   B. violation   C. crime   D. felony

8. According to the above passage, which of the following is classified as a crime?

   A. Offense punishable by 15 days imprisonment
   B. Minor offense
   C. Violation
   D. Misdemeanor

9. According to the above passage, if a person guilty of burglary can receive a prison sentence of 7 years or more, burglary would be classified as a

   A. violation   B. misdemeanor
   C. felony   D. violent act

10. According to the above passage, two offenses that would BOTH be classified as misdemeanors are

    A. making unreasonable noise, and stealing a $90 bicycle
    B. stealing a $75 radio, and possessing 1/16 of an ounce of heroin
    C. holding up a bank, and possessing 1/4 of a pound of marijuana
    D. falsely reporting a fire, and illegally double-parking

11. The above passage says that offenses are classified according to the penalties provided for them.
    On the basis of clues in the passage, who probably decides what the maximum penalties should be for the different kinds of offenses?

    A. The State lawmakers   B. The City police
    C. The Mayor   D. Officials in Washington, D.C.

12. Of the following, which BEST describes the subject matter of the passage?

    A. How society deals with criminals
    B. How offenses are classified
    C. Three types of criminal behavior
    D. The police approach to offenders

Questions 13-20.

DIRECTIONS: Questions 13 through 20 are to be answered SOLELY on the basis of the following passage.

Auto theft is prevalent and costly. In 2005, 486,000 autos valued at over $500 million were stolen. About 28 percent of the inhabitants of Federal prisons are there as a result of conviction of interstate auto theft under the Dyer Act. In California alone, auto thefts cost the criminal justice system approximately $60 million yearly.

The great majority of auto theft is for temporary use rather than resale, as evidenced by the fact that 88 percent of autos stolen in 2005 were recovered. In Los Angeles, 64 percent of stolen autos that were recovered were found within two days, and about 80 percent within a week. Chicago reports that 71 percent of the recovered autos were found within four miles of the point of theft. The FBI estimates that 8 percent of stolen cars are taken for the purpose of stripping them for parts, 12 percent for resale, and 5 percent for use in another crime. Auto thefts are primarily juvenile acts. Although only 21 percent of all arrests for nontraffic offenses in 2005 were of individuals under 18 years of age, 63 percent of auto theft arrests were of persons under 18. Auto theft represents the start of many criminal careers; in an FBI sample of juvenile auto theft offenders, 41 percent had no prior arrest record.

13. In the above passage, the discussion of the reasons for auto theft does NOT include the percent of

    A. autos stolen by prior offenders
    B. recovered stolen autos found close to the point of theft
    C. stolen autos recovered within a week
    D. stolen autos which were recovered

14. Assuming the figures in the above passage remain constant, you may logically estimate the cost of auto thefts to the California criminal justice system over a five-year period beginning in 2005 to have been about _____ million.

    A. $200   B. $300   C. $440   D. $500

15. According to the above passage, the percent of stolen autos in Los Angeles which were not recovered within a week was _____ percent.

    A. 12   B. 20   C. 29   D. 36

16. According to the above passage, MOST auto thefts are committed by

    A. former inmates of Federal prisons   B. juveniles
    C. persons with a prior arrest record   D. residents of large cities

17. According to the above passage, MOST autos are stolen for

    A. resale   B. stripping of parts
    C. temporary use   D. use in another crime

18. According to the above passage, the percent of persons arrested for auto theft who were under 18

    A. equals nearly the same percent of stolen autos which were recovered
    B. equals nearly two-thirds of the total number of persons arrested for nontraffic offenses
    C. is the same as the percent of persons arrested for nontraffic offenses who were under 18
    D. is three times the percent of persons arrested for nontraffic offenses who were under 18

19. An APPROPRIATE title for the above passage is

    A. HOW CRIMINAL CAREERS BEGIN
    B. RECOVERY OF STOLEN CARS
    C. SOME STATISTICS ON AUTO THEFT
    D. THE COSTS OF AUTO THEFT

20. Based on the above passage, the number of cars taken for use in another crime in 2005 was 20.____

    A. 24,300 B. 38,880 C. 48,600 D. 58,320

Questions 21-22.

DIRECTIONS: Questions 21 and 22 are to be answered SOLELY on the basis of the following paragraph.

If the second or third felony is such that, upon a first conviction, the offender would be punishable by imprisonment for any term less than his natural life, then such person must be sentenced to imprisonment for an indeterminate term, the minimum of which shall be not less than one-half of the longest term prescribed upon a first conviction, and the maximum of which shall be not longer than twice such longest term, provided, however, that the minimum sentence imposed hereunder upon such second or third felony offender shall in no case be less than five years; except that where the maximum punishment for a second or third felony offender hereunder is five years or less, the minimum sentence must be not less than two years.

21. According to the above paragraph, a person who has a second felony conviction shall receive as a sentence for that second felony an indeterminate term 21.____

    A. not less than twice the minimum term prescribed upon a first conviction as a maximum
    B. not less than one-half the maximum term of his first conviction as a minimum
    C. not more than twice the minimum term prescribed upon a first conviction as a minimum
    D. with a maximum of not more than twice the longest term prescribed for a first conviction for this crime

22. According to the above paragraph, if the term for this crime for a first offender is up to three years, the possible indeterminate term for this crime as a second or third felony shall have a _____ of not _____ than _____ years. 22.____

    A. minimum; less; five
    B. maximum; more; five
    C. minimum; less; one and one-half
    D. maximum; less; six

23. A statute states: *A person who steals an article worth $1,000 or less where no aggravating circumstances accompany the act is guilty of petit larceny. If the article is worth more than $1,000, it may be grand larceny.*
    If all you know is that Edward Smith stole an article worth $1,000, it may reasonably be said that 23.____

    A. Smith is guilty of petit larceny
    B. Smith is guilty of grand larceny
    C. Smith is guilty of neither petit larceny nor grand larceny
    D. precisely what charge will be placed against Smith is uncertain

Questions 24-25.

DIRECTIONS: Questions 24 and 25 are to be answered on the basis of the following section of a law.

A person who, after having been three times convicted within this state of felonies or attempts to commit felonies, or under the law of any other state, government, or country, of crimes which if committed within this state would be felonious, commits a felony, other than murder, first or second degree, or treason, within this state, shall be sentenced upon conviction of such fourth, or subsequent, offense to imprisonment in a state prison for an indeterminate term the minimum of which shall be not less than the maximum term provided for first offenders for the crime for which the individual has been convicted, but, in any event, the minimum term upon conviction for a felony as the fourth or subsequent, offense shall be not less than fifteen years, and the maximum thereof shall be his natural life.

24. Under the terms of the above law, a person must receive the increased punishment therein provided if

   A. he is convicted of a felony and has been three times previously convicted of felonies
   B. he has been three times previously convicted of felonies, regardless of the nature of his present conviction
   C. his fourth conviction is for murder, first or second degree, or treason
   D. he has previously been convicted three times of murder, first or second degree, or treason

25. Under the terms of the above law, a person convicted of a felony for which the penalty is imprisonment for a term not to exceed ten years, and who has been three times previously convicted of felonies in this state, shall be sentenced to a term, the MINIMUM of which shall be

   A. 10 years   B. 15 years
   C. indeterminate   D. his natural life

KEY (CORRECT ANSWERS)

1.	C	11.	A
2.	B	12.	B
3.	D	13.	A
4.	A	14.	B
5.	C	15.	B
6.	D	16.	B
7.	A	17.	C
8.	D	18.	D
9.	C	19.	C
10.	B	20.	A

21. D
22. C
23. D
24. A
25. B

www.ingramcontent.com/pod-product-compliance
Lightning Source LLC
Chambersburg PA
CBHW082148300426
44117CB00016B/2657